The aim of the *Earth Quest* series is to examine and explain how shamanic principles can be applied in the journey towards self-discovery – and beyond

Each person's Earth quest is the search for meaning and purpose in their life – it is the establishment of identity and the realization of inner potentials and individual responsibility.

Each book in the series examines aspects of a life science that is in harmony with the Earth and shows how each person can attune themselves to nature. Each book imparts knowledge of the Craft of Life.

Shamanic Experience

A PRACTICAL GUIDE TO
SHAMANISM FOR THE NEW MILLENNIUM

Kenneth Meadows, a former journalist and college lecturer, sought answers to some of life's most perplexing questions for more than 30 years. At the point of abandoning his quest he came into contact with shamans and medicine men – the 'wise' ones of indigenous peoples – who pointed him to the Book of Nature for instruction and to the need to look within rather than to an outside source for the answers he sought.

He was shown how to traverse 'inner' space and was given the 'medicine' name *Flying Horse* – meaning 'communicator of other realms' – and encouraged to share this knowledge through the writing of books. *Shamanic Experience* is one of five books Kenneth has written in Element's *Earth Quest* series.

Kenneth harmonises Medicine Wheel principles of native Americans with shamanic concepts of other races and cultures world-wide to provide a *universal* shamanism for the new millennium, freeing ancient wisdom from tribal and racial limitations and superstitions and applying its eternal principles to modern times where it can be both practical and relevant to everyday life today and wherever we happen to be. This unique process of personal development expands human consciousness, extends the senses, furthers human potential, and improves the quality of life.

Shamanic Experience is a practical hand-book for the exploration of your inner space, activating abilities that lie dormant, and finding guidance from a source of wisdom to be found *within*.

By the same author

Shamanic Experience

A PRACTICAL GUIDE TO SHAMANISM
FOR THE NEW MILLENNIUM

Kenneth Meadows

ELEMENT
Shaftesbury, Dorset • Boston, Massachusetts
Melbourne, Victoria

© Element Books Limited 1991
Text © Kenneth Meadows 1991

First published in the UK in 1991 by
Element Books Limited
Shaftesbury, Dorset SP7 8BP

Published in the USA in 1991 by
Element Books, Inc.
160 North Washington Street
Boston, MA 02114

Published in Australia in 1997 by
Element Books and distributed
by Penguin Australia Limited
487 Maroondah Highway, Ringwood,
Victoria 3134

Reprinted 1992
Reprinted 1993
Reprinted 1994
Reprinted 1995
Reprinted February and December 1996

Reissued 1998

Cover design by Max Fairbrother
Typeset by Bournemouth Colour Press, Parkstone, Poole, Dorset
Printed and bound in Great Britain by J.W. Arrowsmith Limited, Bristol

British Library Cataloguing in Publication
data available

Library of Congress Cataloging in Publication
data available

ISBN 1 85230 226 7

CONTENTS

Acknowledgements

The Commission

PRACTICAL EXERCISES

Acknowledgements

THIS BOOK WOULD NOT HAVE BEEN POSSIBLE without the inspiration and guidance of my principal mentor, Medicine Chief Silver Bear, and the help and advice I have received from shamans and students of shamanism in Britain, America, Europe, and Scandinavia. And it could not have been completed without the patience, understanding and constructive advice of my wife, Beryl, who has shared with me not only the adventure of life but also the wonders of the shamanic experience and the teachings of her mentor.

THE COMMISSION GIVEN TO 'FLYING HORSE' BY THE MYSTIC MEDICINE CHIEF 'SILVER BEAR'.

When you walk in darkness
It is no use carrying a lantern
Whose light cannot be seen.
For, then, every step you take
Will be a hesitation into the unknown
Where any tiny pebble on the Path
May cause you to trip or stumble,
Or the slightest impediment,
A cause for you to give up
And abandon the journey
To try, perhaps, another path.
So make a lantern,
Lit from the Red Indian fire
And whose light shines clear
For the way you've come
To be seen and marked,
And the way ahead to hold no fear
For others who come after you
To walk with an assurance,
Seeing by light from a torch you have left.
For those who walk this Path
Should not be left to grope in the dark
When light can make them aware
That the Path is beautiful
And the steps they take
Can be a choreography of beauty, too.
For this Path is the Beauty Way, the beautiful way,
Where all who will may Dance in Beauty
Around their own hearth fire
What they need to light the Way
Is a lantern that is bright.
So make one.
Lit from the torch you have been given.
The eight-rayed Torch,
The Flame Within
That illuminates the Eight Directions
And the Eight Dimensions.
Make one.
Be a Sun, Grandfather.

(This book is a component of that 'lantern'.)

The New Frontier

IN AN AGE WHEN much of the Earth's surface has already been explored, mankind feels a need to satisfy an inherent spirit of adventure, and experience the thrill of discovery by going beyond the Earth to unexplored regions outside the atmosphere of the planet, into what has been called Outer Space. But there is another frontier, hitherto neglected, unheard of or overlooked by most, but experienced by some. It is as challenging as the space travel of astronauts, yet it requires no expenditure of vast sums of money, no rigorous training to tax the physical body to its limits, and it need not be confined to a special few. It is readily available to all, and is richly rewarding in terms of self-development and the personal benefits its exploration can bring.

It is the non-physical realm of the shamanist. A shamanist is a person who, by applying the spiritual principles of the shaman, is enabled to experience the extra-ordinary whilst living an ordinary life in a modern society.

To the shamanist, space is not an empty 'nothing', no vast expanse of 'emptiness' as we have supposed. Space is 'something' and has certain qualities, in the same way as a physical substance. And space exists not only around things and between things but also *within* things for, as science has discovered, physical matter which has the appearance of solidity is not 'solid' after all but is composed of atoms which themselves consist largely of space. This 'space within' can be explored and experienced. It is the realm of the shamanist – an explorer not of some some far-off plant in Outer Space, but of the non-physical existence of worlds within – of Inner Space.

Through this exploration the shamanist is able to perceive what others cannot see, and to expand and extend the consciousness so that realities can be experienced that are beyond the physical appearances of ordinary everyday life. In this realm of the 'non-ordinary' the shamanist finds that time also is not what it seems. Time is not constant, as is supposed, but 'elastic' and can be stretched or contracted like a rubber band. In this new dimension the shaman experiences an awareness that penetrates the constraints of the physical and goes beyond the logic of the mind (for it transcends the intellect, too). But before we examine the world of the shamanist, let us first establish what a shaman is.

Anthropologists and ethnologists have concluded that shamans have figured in human affairs since way back beyond recorded history. Ethnologists believe that shamans originated from the peoples of Central and North Asia, whose spiritual life appeared to centre around their shaman – a person who could influence their lives through presumed contact with the 'hidden' forces of Nature.

Michael Harner, a renowned American anthropologist in his classic work *The Way of the Shaman*, says the word 'shaman' (pronounced 'shahmahn') is derived from the language of the Tungus people of Siberia. It can be translated as meaning 'to work with heat and fire; to heat or burn up'. So the word as applied to a person may be taken to mean 'a transformer of energy', because fire is not only energy but also an agent of change. Since a shaman was considered to be one who was able to make the greatest transformation of all – from the physical to the spiritual – that is quite an apt definition.

In some dictionaries the word 'shaman' is described as 'a wise person' or 'one who knows', but these are rather incomplete definitions. The word more precisely means 'one who knows *ecstasy*', because it is an ecstatic experience that singles out the shaman: the experience of obtaining information, guidance, help, advice, healing and empowerment as a result of connecting to an inner power that is inherent within all things. For it is an experience of another reality, one that is beyond the laws of physics and chemistry a reality of the spirit from which the reality of matter is derived.

A shamanist is one who understands that life is in everything and that there are many ways of experiencing it. Being human is only one of them. A shamanist perceives that other life forms – an animal, a bird, a fish, an inset, a tree – experience life for what it is, and from their own particular perspectives. A shamanist, treats everything with respect and learns to recognize the essential spirit of life in all things. In so doing he* comes to understand himself and the interdependence of all things.

A shamanist recognizes that man is privileged for he has the power to change or shape things at will. Take an example: a diamond forms deep in the Earth over a period of many thousands of years. It cannot move of its own volition and must stay where it is, forever hidden away. Man can choose to dig in the Earth and find the diamond and bring it into the light. He can clean it, shape it, and polish it, and in so doing bring new experiences to the diamond that it could in no way have done for itself. The diamond could then be set in a ring and put on the finger of a woman where it would experience its life in close relationship with a human, even

*Though I use the male pronominal form in referring to the shaman, it should be clearly understood that a shaman may be either male or female.

to the point of absorbing her vibrations. In return for this wealth of experience, what does the diamond do? It gives of its brilliant beauty to all who see it. It gives confidence and pleasure to its wearer because of its own inherent qualities and indestructible value.

A shamanist learns to see every aspect of life in this light – that everything is interdependent and mutually supportive – thereby coming into harmony with all things. This can only lead to an understanding that we are of the Earth and dependent on the Earth for our survival, and that the Earth itself is a living being – an organism within the greater organism of the universe.

As the shamanist's understanding increases he recognizes that the essence of all life is unseen – it belongs to another reality as well as the physical. Just as man can bring new experiences to the diamond and establish a spirit of harmony between the diamond and human life, so that effort put into recognizing the spirit of life in all things is rewarded by that spirit revealing itself to the shaman. As a result he becomes aware of realities other than the ordinary, and knowledge of these gives him a very deep and true understanding of the everyday world. The spirit of all life opens doors for the shamanist to experience these other realities and other perspectives, and shows how he can use these experiences for the benefit of himself and others.

The word 'shaman' has also been defined as 'one who walks between the worlds' and this, too, is a meaningful interpretation because it identifies the shaman with different kinds of reality. These various 'worlds' co-exist with that of the ordinary, physical one. Indeed they interpenetrate it, but remain hidden from what can be physically seen and sensed because they exist in other dimensions. These other 'worlds' cannot be reached by being rocketed great distances into Outer Space over vast periods of time, but only by being projected into the dimension of Inner Space where time has little or no relevance.

Just as the physical realm contains different 'kingdoms' – mineral, plant, animal, and human – so these other 'worlds' are on different levels or wavelengths of existence. Shamanists can extend the boundaries of their awareness by transferring their consciousness to these inner worlds by techniques of spirit travel or Soul journeying. They are empowered to perform certain work through spirit travel to a 'lower' world of subconscious reality, and to acquire inspiration and knowledge through Soul journeys to an 'upper' world of superconscious reality. They are carried on these journeys by the Life Force and is able to communicate with any life forms he encounters just as he is able to converse with the different life forms of the physical world – with animals, trees, and even rocks and stones, for instance, How? By making contact with the Life

Force – the intelligence within them – with their 'spirit'. Such contact can be made because the human spirit and the spirit of all living things are manifestations of the same Life Force and are all, therefore, interconnected. For instance, a tree and a shaman use the same Life Force but their individualities organize it in different ways to follow the Laws of their own being.

Everything thus has its role in this holistic scheme of things, and its place in relation to everything in existence. The shamanist finds that non-human forms of life are inherently 'aware' both of their place and their purpose, and operate in an instinctive and automative sense within the limitations imposed upon them by Cosmic Law. Humans, however, feel no such constraints and operate in accordance with free will, and so need to discover this sense of place and purpose.

The word 'shamanism' has become quite fashionable among people with an interest in mysticism and so-called New Age thinking and life-enhancement systems. It is misleading to use the word as a synonym for 'occult', or as a name for a Nature-worship religion, or an esoteric cult. It is none of these things. By definition shamanism is the study and practice of the principles and techniques of shamans. It is concerned with the interrelationship of one's own Life Force with the spirit of anything and everything else, be it human, animal, plant, mineral or celestial; the individuality *within* reaching out to the 'within' of everything else.

Shamanism connects the individual with Nature and with other levels of existence and in so doing seeks not to manipulate, control, or exploit, but rather to engage the willing co-operation and active support of all forms of life in a mutual endeavour of self-development and growth which is spiritual evolution. Shamanism is thus, by its very nature, highly individualistic.

Shamanism thus has nothing to do with the so-called supernatural because it is essentially a natural and holistic activity. It recognizes that everything is an energy-system in itself within a greater Energy-System, and therefore linked to the energy-systems of everything else, so deserving respect because each plays a part in the great Cosmic scheme of things. So shamanism is no 'new' religion, or even a revival of an 'old' one. Indeed, it is not a belief system at all for it propagates no doctrines. It rests not on faith but on the acquisition of experienced knowledge – that is, knowledge that can be attained by the individual. A difference between a religionist and a shamanist is that a religious person's concept of Truth is based upon faith in the word or authority of another and depends upon the interpretation given to those words, whether oral or written. A shamanist's concept of Truth is based upon personal experience. A religious person believes that realms do exist beyond the normal physical existence and, indeed, hope of a future life depends upon it. A shamanist knows such realms exist because he has experienced them for himself in an altered state of consciousness.

In shamanism neither faith nor intellectual prowess are prerequisites. In shamanism you simply *do* it in order to *know* it; knowledge comes through the *doing*. There is no set of beliefs to be accepted before progress can be made; no dogma or creed to be bound by; no sacred writings to be revered and interpreted, literalized or allegorized; no hierarchy to demand devotion; no vows to be sworn. Only the power source that is within to be awakened and guidelines needed to point the way.

How is it that so little is generally known about shamanism among technologically advanced and well-educated nations? One reason is that the knowledge of its teachings was suppressed during the centuries of religious intolerance and bigotry. Another is that they became 'forgotten' or 'lost' through the political, industrial and social changes which urbanized our ancestors and disconnected them from their shamanic roots. Today most of us living in an industrialized society have little communication with Nature and the environment, and no contact with the life pulse of the planet Earth itself. The consequences of this ignorance are now all too evident. The ecology is gravely damaged, and whole species of animals and plants are becoming extinct. Even the plant itself is threatened and, of course, with it the survival of the human race.

Many of our most pressing environmental problems are the result of personal imbalance on a massive scale. The Earth itself is now suffering as a result of mankind's ignorance and reckless exploitation. The equilibrium can only be regained through a renewed respect for Nature, the Earth and for all its inhabitants, whether human or non-human. So this ancient understanding has never been more relevant to the needs of ordinary people than it is today.

How can we reconnect with this 'lost' or 'forgotten' shamanic knowledge? How can it be regained? An insight into American Indian spirituality and its principal methodology – the Medicine Wheel – is one way, principally because American Indians are historically nearer their shamanic roots than we are to ours. The shamanic wisdom of the native American remained essentially the same for thousands of years, deeply rooted in the Earth and in tune with Nature, unlike the mystical traditions of some other cultures which underwent changes through the influence of the world's monotheistic religions. The Medicine Wheel also provides an effective means of finding one's way into the holistic and multi-dimensional system of the Cosmos.

To the American Indian, 'medicine' more than a substance to soothe and heal the physical body. 'Medicine' implied the knowledge and power that brought harmony and balance to every life form. Knowledge was interpreted not just as information, but as that which provided an inner knowing – inner truth. Power was understood as energized force which was able to perform particular work. So the Medicine Wheel might be defined as 'a circle of knowledge which provides the ability to perform work which produces harmony and balance'.

The knowledge to which the Medicine Wheel provides access enables its users not only to find direction in life but also in other dimensions of existence. It can therefore be regarded as a shamanic map, as well as a device for understanding physical, mental and spiritual realities. The native shamanism of Britain and Northern Europe used a similar circular mandala, though it became obscured through the imposition of supernatural concepts as a result of alien religious ideas.

A shamanic approach is more effective than philosophical systems because it operates within natural and cosmic laws and is part of Nature with its seasonal and cyclical energy patterns. Freed from ritualistic practices and superstitious beliefs which were imposed upon them, these *universal* shamanic principles provide a way of effective living in a modern age. I have called this distillation of ancient wisdom *Shamanics* to distinguish it from the regurgitations of ritualistic practices and superstitious beliefs which have become part of 'contemporary' shamanism. *Shamanics* is shamanism re-newed. It is the 'new' shamanism – a Science of the Spirit for the new millennium.

Shamanics is neither a religion nor a cult. But it does embrace several important understandings:

First: Establishing contact with the Spirit *within* – one's *own* spirit – as the source of personal empowerment and creativity rather than a dependence on some outside power or authority or external spirits of whatever kind.

Second: We are each a Spirit with a body, a mind and a soul and not a body and mind with a spirit and a soul. The Spirit is the essence of what we *are* and is the essential 'I' and not the mortal self. At death the Spirit withdraws its life from the physical body.

Third: Everything is alive. Everything vibrates: animals, trees, plants – even rocks. Each is a part of the lives of one another, and each has it own life which itself is inherently an expression of the Supreme Intelligence which brought it into existence. Each is organized differently from human life, service a specific purpose for which it was designed. And each has an awareness very different from that of humans, but it is an 'awareness' all

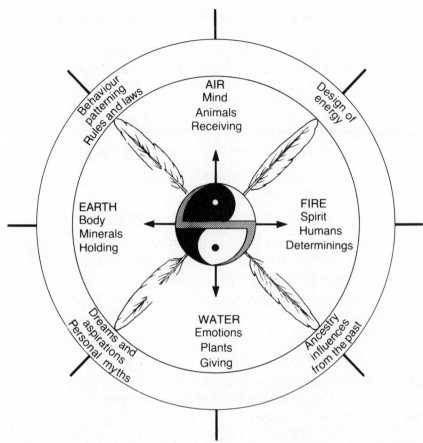

Fig 1. A Medicine Wheel adaptation as a shamanic map for finding direction in life and for aligning physical, mental and spiritual realities

the same. This understanding, once recognized, changes one's attitude to the Earth and its environment.

Fourth: There are inner zones of reality which affect and regulate what we experience outwardly. And within these inner realms are helpers, guides and teachers with power to effect change in the outer reality.

Those of us who have been brought up in a modern society, influenced by materialistic science and monotheistic religion, have been conditioned to accept that we live in a three-dimensional world. Our experience of reality is based on what is perceived through the five physical sense, on what can be 'proved' or demonstrated by observation, and by what can be concluded through lateral thought which we call logic.

In this conditioned thinking, everything must have a beginning and an ending, and every effect must have a cause. Western culture is materialistically oriented in spite of its religious undertones. It assumes that mankind lives in an unfriendly environment which has to be controlled and subjugated, and that the Earth itself exists in a hostile universe, far from any intelligent life that may exist elsewhere. Its deity is male, who is either outside and separate from his Creation or who had entered it in human form.

A shamanist operates in accordance with a different perspective:

- Man is not alone but interrelated with all life forms with which the Earth environment is shared.

- Nothing in being exists in isolation; everything is connected.

- There is a Supreme Intelligence behind all things in existence – which American Indian shamans called the Great Spirit – and it is not outside but inside Creation.

- The Great Spirit limited its expression within Sacred Laws, and therefore limited Him/Her/Itself. All thus evolved within the Law of its own being.

- All power comes from within.

Clearly, then, in order to experience shamanics for yourself it is necessary to set aside conventional beliefs and maintain an open mind. This does not mean abandoning religious faith or philosophical convictions, just putting aside for the time being preconceived ideas so that shamanic principles may be approached in a receptive manner, and a shamanic perspective experienced.

Through an understanding of shamanics you can then:

- Comprehend forces and energies that exist beyond the range of the physical senses and learn to work with them.

- Become aware of your own non-physical dimensions and those of all beings, whether human, animal, plant or mineral.

- Develop an inner vision that will enable you to comprehend the inner planes of existence and affect what is coming into manifestation from the realm of the unmanifest.

- Develop an insight into people's characters and an understanding of the technology of personality construction through the shamanic knowledge of Earth Medicine.

- Develop practical skills in personality profiling, oracular counselling, divination and distant healing.

- Shift your consciousness to different planes of existence.

- Free yourself from unwanted restrictions and limitations.

- Release yourself from the illusions of false beliefs which can inhibit and enslave you.

- Discover personal gateways to greater power and mastery over your life.

- Learn to cope with difficulties in your life which are hindering your progress, and avoid obstacles which might be hard to overcome.

- Broaden your perspective of life.

- Absorb the healing energies of the universe and become more efficient, more receptive, and more responsive.

- Learn the language of the subconscious mind and of the 'Hidden' self and work with natural images and symbols.

- Develop an inner hearing so you can listen to the voices of Nature.

- Discover your hidden potentials and develop your creativity.

- Activate your imagination and bring your dreams and aspirations into practical reality.

- Take charge of your own life and cease to be a victim of circumstance.

- Improve your personal relationships.

- Come into harmony with the Earth and with Earth energies and align with the Cosmic forces of the universe.

Traditionally, a tribal shaman become initiated through rigorous and often savage tests, after a long apprenticeship. He was either chosen by an experienced shaman, or had inherited the role from a parent or grandparent. Historically, some shamans were self-selected, sometimes after undergoing a near-death or mystical experience, or through inner conviction. In the New Age which is just dawning, shamanic understanding is not to be the limited province of a 'special' few, but will be openly available to all.

This book, therefore, is not intended as a training manual for novice shamans, but as a practical guide to shamanic techniques but can be used by anyone anywhere as a means of solving personal problems, eliminating difficulties, removing obstructions to individual progress, becoming more efficient and creative, and living a more enriched, harmonious and fulfilling life.

Although there are different shamanic approaches to an understanding of the Cosmos which have been largely conditioned by tribal customs, cultural traditions, and racial ancestry, there are recognizable similarities. In attempting to present a shamanic perspective of life that is relevant to those of us living in a modern urban society, I have approached these concepts in the spirit of the wandering shaman. The wandering shaman was one who travelled beyond his own tribal and sometimes racial boundaries, seeking Truth wherever it could be found, weaving what he learned with what was already known, and conveying understanding to all who had ears to hear and eyes to see.

CHAPTER TWO

Tuning the Senses

THE POWER TO DO SHAMANIC WORK is both within you and outside you and is readily accessible for channelling through you. Your inner resources include the creative power of thought and imagination, and the driving force of your spirit energy. They provide vitality, strength and determination, a supply of individual potentials which, however dormant or neglected, can be awakened, and your own well of wisdom from which to obtain direction and inspiration. These inner resources constitute your power, or what American Indian shamans called 'medicine'.

The outside forces are none other than the Powers of the Universe that are contained within a great web of energies, in which everything that exists has life and is interconnected through its Life Force, and in which all are mutually supportive.

For spirit *is* the Life Force. It is the invisible essence of whatever is manifested. It is the power that is flowing through every living thing and which provides the energy for it to express its separate identity. But although spirit flows through all forms it is largely 'unknown' because it is hidden behind the apparent physical 'appearance' of things. Modern science has no knowledge of the true nature of spirit because, unlike matter, it cannot be seen or measured. It is so elusive that it cannot be dissected by the logical mind either, because it transcends the intellect. Spirit is 'nothing' yet, paradoxically, it is in everything and everything is in it. Modern science has an inadequate and incomplete understanding of the nature of man and of life itself because it tends to be concerned solely with the physical, and ignores the spiritual, assigning it to the province of the theologian where it has rested on 'faith' and belief in the supernatural. Yet spirit, and how to live within it, was known to shamans before any organized religion or man-made philosophy determined what was and was not to be believed or experienced, and laid down that the knowledge would be available only through a privileged priesthood. Spirit, once unveiled, opens up a whole new realm of experience. Living is no longer a perplexity of chance and coincidence, but takes on real meaning and purpose.

We have all been brainwashed – conditioned by society and culture and materialistic science and its technology – to look little further than beyond our noses. We have been manipulated into believing that the Earth is a huge globe of inanimate matter – just a chunk of rock orbiting through space. Minerals within it are there to be taken; trees are timber with which to make paper; animals are flesh and bones, to be hunted or factory-farmed for food, or to be experimented on.

Shamans have always had a different perspective. They see everything in existence as having purpose and being charged with power – pulsating with life – and the source of that power as being spiritual, not material. The shaman knows from personal experience that it is possible to connect with that power through the spirit within him. It is because of the reality of that communication that the shaman has such a deep respect for all things, and an understanding of the workings of Nature and of the Universe.

So nothing is as it appears. What seems to be solid, physical reality is, in fact, a complex system of vibrating energies. What our eyes actually see are dancing patterns that we recognize as objects or as other living creatures.

We are connected with what we can see by pulsating waves of light-energy which cause electrical impulses on the retina of the eye which are sent to the brain to be interpreted as visual images. This is just one way in which we are linked by fibres of energy other things, like the strands of a spider's web. Everything in existence consists of energies organized in a particular way. These energies may be likened to complex radio waves consisting of many different frequencies. Our normal physical senses enable us to tune in to some of these frequencies; they provide 'windows' through which we sense certain energy patterns. Those sources that are vibrating at rates faster or slower than our sensual register can accept are beyond our physical reach. We cannot see them, hear them, smell, touch, taste or feel them, and so we are lead to believe that they do not exist.

A shamanist is able to tune in to some of these 'hidden' energies and be sensitive to things that most people cannot detect. This is achieved in two principal ways. First, by making fuller use of the physical senses so that one is aware of vibrations of energy that are beyond the normal range. Second, by awakening and exercising 'inner' receptors that are dormant in most people and which enable one to reach other 'worlds' – other dimensions of reality, or spiritual energy-bands – and their laws, and the beings within them. I shall be describing in Chapter 7 techniques that can help you to experience these spiritual realities for yourself.

So you don't have to be 'psychic' to become a shamanist, but in doing so you extend the range of your senses and develop abilities which some people might regard as 'psychic'.

How do you extend the senses so they become what is generally regarded as extra-sensory? Firstly, by working on the 'ordinary' physical senses. Most of us, brought up in an industrialized society, make such poor use of these that relatively speaking we are half-blind, half-deaf, and so unfeeling that we are less than half-alive. We see enough to stop us from bumping into things, or hear a vehicle, thereby preventing us from being run over, and limit ourselves to feeling what is immediately to hand. Test our powers of observation and most of us would score poorly. I am frequently asked if there are exercises that can extend, say, the range of vision. I am sure there are tedious eye exercises; but there is a more effective way that will benefit your entire energy-system, and that is simply to get involved with the world of Nature. So here is your first practical exercise.

EXERCISE 1: Stretching your eyes

This exercise entails taking a walk or even a journey, for it is necessary to get away from the comfort and constraints of your home and into the countryside. If you live in a town or a city it may involve a journey by a car or public transport. But it is a necessary part of your shamanic training to get away from being boxed in by four walls and from the concrete jungle of civilization, from the noise of traffic and the busying of people about their daily chores, and to be absorbed in Nature for a while. You need to find a place in open countryside where you can be alone to 'stretch your eyes' by observing the panorama all around you. Don't hurry the experience. Allow your senses to wallow in the enjoyment of it all. Focus your eyes on some interesting point on the horizon, and then on something close to you and within easy reach. Let your eyes enjoy the freedom of exploration.

Then take a walk across fields or into woodland. Let your eyes search for wild flowers or fruit, nuts or fungi that may be in season. Pause frequently to stand still and just watch and listen and let your senses delight in their freedom. Then sit and listen to Nature. Try to hear the slightest of sounds; identify their direction and tune in to them. Really 'feel' the Earth by reaching out with all your senses and savour its smells, its 'taste', its 'touch'.

Do this and you will discover it to be more than an exercise to tune the senses. It will relax the whole mind and body and act as a tonic to invigorate your entire energy-system. And like a good tonic it should be taken regularly!

Evidence of an extension of the frequency range of the senses is usually an ability to feel or see auras. The word 'aura' is derived from a Greek word which means 'breeze', for an aura is a bio-plasmic energy field which surrounds a life form and, like a breeze, is in a state of constant motion and change, and is usually unseen because its frequencies are beyond the limits of normal eyesight. The aura of a human being is composed of a complex network of gossamer-like energy threads which are structured like the fibres of a feather and surround the physical body like a fibrous cocoon. It extends both in front of and behind the physical body, and above the head and beneath the feet, and is not unlike a huge egg standing upright.

An extension of the frequency range of the eyesight can sometimes be triggered by the way one looks at things. The trick here is to look at the spaces *between* things, rather than at the person or object directly. A way to achieve this is simply to stare at the person and then to relax the gaze and let the eyes go out of focus – as if you are looking through him rather than at him. You can get the idea by looking at yourself in a mirror. Sit in a room with subdued lighting and stay at the mirror long enough for the conscious mind to 'switch off'. Don't focus on on your reflection. Be very aware of what is seen with the peripheral vision.

EXERCISE 2:   Seeing the aura

Obtain a piece of pale blue card or stiff material. Hold your hand, with fingers splayed, about 30–40 cm in front of you and 8–10 cm from the background material. If you now gaze at the background as if through your hand, you should see a thin, blue haze extending around the edges of your fingers and hand. It may look like thin blue smoke, forming a clear outline. This is the Energy Body that takes on roughly the shape of the physical body and forms part of the aura.

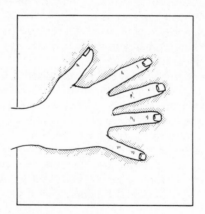

Fig 2. Seeing the aura

Get a friend or partner to stand some distance away from you and with an unobtrusive background behind them. Fix your gaze on the whole person, then relax your eyes and let them go out of focus as if you were looking right through him. You may have to practise this technique a few times before you become aware of a shadowy haze around the figure, not unlike the glow around the children in a popular television commercial which advertises a certain breakfast cereal. This is the aura. If you try to focus your eyes on it the auric glow is likely to vanish, so you must learn to analyse what you are seing whilst your eyes are still fixed in a stare. Is the size and shape changing as you look? What is its predominant colour? Can you distinguish other colours? Is its fogginess becoming clearer? Write down your impressions immediately while they are still fresh in your mind. It is sensible to keep a record of your shamanic training work so this is a good way to start it.

Ask your companion to conduct the same exercise, with you as the subject, and compare results. Practise this way of sensing or seeing for a few minutes regularly over the next few days and make notes of your experiences each time. In due course you will assess the aura more extensively and in greater detail as your ability develops.

On sunny days when there is much energy in the air, auras can be sensed or seen more easily. Ensure you are relaxed and calm. The secret is not to try too hard!

The shaman not only makes use of extended vision but fine tunes the senses of hearing and touch also. So in addition to seeing an aura we need to be able to feel it, and most people find this easier. Here is a set of experiments you can do on your own or with a partner to develop an auric feel.

EXERCISE 3:   Feeling the human aura

Hold your left hand upright just in front of you and your right hand horizontally, with the tips of your fingers about 3 or 4 cm (an inch or so) from your left hand. Move the fingers very slowly up and down across the palm. In this way you are drawing your hand through that part of the aura that is nearest the body. The aura will feel like a slight tingling sensation across the palm, or like a soft breeze. Other more subtle layers of the aura may be felt by moving the hands away from the temples outwards. Definite changes in vibrational rate can be felt.

Another method is to sit with your hands in front of you so the tips of the fingers are close but without actually touching. If you feel a sensation like brushing through body hair, this is your auric energy.

If you have a partner, try this third method:

Have your partner stand facing a mirror about 50 cm (a couple of feet) away. Stand behind your partner and ask him or her to close their eyes and tell you the moment they feel your fingers touching their hair. Hold your hands, palms down and slightly cupped, about 30 cm (a foot or so) above the head. Now lower your hands very slowly until you feel a slight and gentle pressure, almost like the springy softness of touching hair. It is likely that your partner will say you are touching his or her head when, in fact, your fingers have stopped at the springy pressure area just above the head. That pressure you feel will be the surface of the aura, and your partner will have a sensation as if you were touching the hair or skin. Keep your hands where they are, and ask your partner to open his eyes. You may both be surprised by this little experiment.

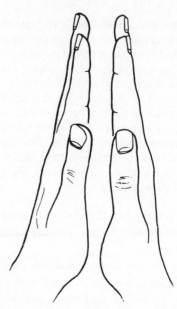

Fig 3. Feeling auric energy

In these simple preliminary exercises a key to success is the ability to relax, and relaxation is a vital ingredient of any shamanic work. The shaman uses it to release tension and to slow down the heartbeat. Since the physical control system then has less to do, energy can be released to expand the mind and the vision. Relaxation slows the train of thought flowing through the brain, and this is essential for the brain circuits to switch to the lower Alpha pattern which shifts the emphasis from left-lobe logical, analytical and sequential functioning to right-lobe intuitive, holistic and creative activity.

Shamanic relaxation is a technique of letting go. For most of us who live in a high-pressure modern society it entails more than physical relaxation of the muscles, for the stress we suffer is not so much the result of physical exertion, but of emotional and mental pressures. This type of relaxation entails more than just pushing aside work worries, romantic difficulties, family problems, and the cares and concerns of everyday life: it requires letting them go. For these everyday concerns have found physical expression – in the tightness of the lips and eyes, in the digestive system, and in various aches and pains – and only by releasing these emotional and mental hang-ups can the muscles of the body relax properly.

The true purpose of relaxation for the shamanic adventurer is to *expand the consciousness*. Do you want to see and hear and feel energies which have so far been outside the range of your experience? In order to attain this shamanic state you must be relaxed, in a state of calm receptivity, distanced from the chatter and clatter of mundane activity, where no demands are being made upon you and where you may be aware instead of internal communications. It is to increase *awareness* that the shaman relaxes. It is the light of consciousness which carries information within a realm of existence or from one level of being to another. Awareness is primarily a function of the spirit. When passive it is receptive. When active it engages in what is called 'thinking'. Ability to perceive non-ordinary realities is attained through passive awareness – by just observing; just being aware.

So let us practise the technique of relaxation – of simply letting go.

EXERCISE 4:   Letting go

You must be physically comfortable before you can relax properly, and posture is important. It is not necessary to adopt cross-legged yogic positions unless you have already been trained in them. Either lie on your back on the floor or sit in a straight-backed chair. Lying down is best because this is the preferred position for shamanic journeying, which we shall be examining in Chapter 7. Lie on a blanket or sleeping bag and use a cushion, pillow, or some other support for your head so that you do not suffer a stiff neck afterwards. If you prefer being seated, avoid an armchair or a seat that's too comfortable. A chair with a high back is best because this gives lumbar support and helps to avoid a tendency to slump forward during the exercise. The spine should be kept straight to allow the energies to flow easily and correctly. If you do choose a sitting position, take your shoes off and make sure the soles of your feet are flat on the floor.

It is best to cover the eyes with a headscarf or handkerchief to avoid any visual distractions. The kind of eye-shield supplied by some airlines for passengers who want to enjoy a nap on night flights is ideal.

This relaxation exercise is simply a matter of tensing the muscles in each part of the body in turn, starting with the feet and working up to the head, and then relaxing them after a few seconds. This tensing and relaxing should be done rhythmically along with the breathing.

So, take a deep breath by pushing out the abdomen, and as you do so count to four seconds: 'In . . . two . . . three . . . four.' Hold the breath and tense the muscles of your feet and count to four seconds: 'Hold . . . two . . . three . . . four.' Exhale slowly to a count of four: 'Out . . . two . . . three . . . four' and as you do so let your toes relax. Then pause to a count of four seconds: 'Pause . . . two . . . three . . . four' and enjoy the sensation of relaxed feet.

Breathe in to four, hold the breath, then as you pause for four seconds tense the muscles of the calves. As you exhale let go of the tension in your calves. Pause for four seconds and enjoy the sensation of relaxed calves.

Now repeat this procedure for the thighs, abdomen, chest, arms, hands, shoulders, neck, face and scalp. Take care not to overtense the abdomen and stomach muscles as this produces extra tension, and is Nature's way of triggering the release of adrenalin. When you have completed relaxing the scalp, breathe normally and just enjoy the feeling of being total, like soaking in a warm bath. End the exercise by having a good stretch, pushing your arms and legs as far as they will go, and taking a deep breath.

This combined relaxation-and-rhythmic-breathing exercise will have beneficial side-effects when performed regularly over a period of time. You will feel calmer and more able to cope with stressful pressures; you will be more patient and considerate, more aware, and will find it easier to concentrate.

Having learned to relax we can now discover how our perception is being expanded by extending our awareness of the human aura to other living things. Let us begin with a tree, because trees are among the most powerful of 'helpers' to the shaman.

American Indian shamans regarded trees as 'the standing people', and a tree as a thought in the mind of the Great Spirit expressing itself *in one place*. A tree stays where it is and draws its sustenance from the sun, rain and wind, and from the mineral kingdom of the soil in which it is rooted. So, as well as expressing its own special characteristics, a tree also contributes to the expression of the quality of the place in which it is planted.

Shamans of all cultures recognized the value of trees, not only because of their beauty and for their contribution to the ecology as the 'lungs' of the Earth, but also as 'teachers' and 'guardians' of humanity. It is significant that the living form used by Nordic and European shamans to obtain access to Other-world realities was a tree. Symbolically the tree is seen as linking Earth to Heaven.

Our next exercise is to experience the aura of a tree and to absorb power from that tree into our own energy-system, so supplementing and strengthening it.

EXERCISE 5:   Drawing power from a tree

Go outdoors and find a tree, in your garden, in a nearby park, or in a field or woodland. It must be somewhere you can sit quietly for half an hour or so without interruption or interference. Choose preferably an oak, silver birch or ash tree, because all of these have strong and vibrant auras. If you are unsure about what these trees look like, go to your public library and consult a book that enables you to identify them easily.

When you have found your tree, talk to it orally or mentally! Words are your means of communication at present, but mix emotion with the words you use, and really mean what you are saying. Tell it you admire its beauty and magnificence. Tell it you are its friend. Tell it you would like to experience its aura and ask it to reveal it to you. Don't concern yourself about what other people might think: other people aren't with you, so it is a matter only between you and the tree. After all, what is so strange about communicating with another living being?

You will know whether it is right to continue. If you feel uncomfortable in any way, go to another tree and try again. When you sense a positive response, sit under the tree with your back firmly against its trunk and simply r-e-l-a-x. Put into practice the relaxation and rhythmic breathing procedure you learned in the last exercise. Then, breathing normally, concentrate your mind on sensing the aura of the tree and being energized by it. You don't have to 'try': it requires no effort. Again, just ask the tree: 'Please help me to sense your aura and to share its energy.' Mean it. Then just relax. You will recognize the feeling when it comes — like soaking in a bath. A comfortable, warm, glowing sensation as your aura merges with that of the tree. You may even become aware of a greenish, hazy glow around you. Should this happen, your vision has been expanded so that you are actually seeing the tree's aura extending into your own.

Take time with this exercise. Don't hurry it in any way, or get impatient if nothing seems to be happening. Spend at least half an hour with your tree, and if you don't experience a positive response at the first attempt, try again another day. Be patient, persistent and considerate, and the response will come.

Before leaving the site, thank the tree. Take with you a little cornmeal, rubbed sage or mixed herbs, and sprinkle them around the base of the tree trunk as a 'thank you'.

Since you are going to be doing some of your shamanic work in natural surroundings it is worth obtaining a little pouch in which to carry such an offering. This exchange of energy is an important principle of shamanism: one never takes without giving. For far too long mankind has taken from Nature and given little or nothing in return. If you want to gain the trust and co-operation of Nature-beings you need to demonstrate that your attitude is one of mutual respect, and not exploitation. Such an attitude will be well rewarded in due course.

Shamanism, then, is an activity of the whole Being. It is concerned with the interchange of your spirit — the very essence of your being — with that of everything else. My principal mentor, Medicine Chief Silver Bear, put it to me this way:

It is only through the spirit that you can come into contact with the Life Forces of rocks and plants and animals who will be your allies, and with the ancestors and enlightened souls and higher Cosmic beings who will be your helpers. For the spirit is the being. It is *be*-ing. It is *be-ing* that which is in the process of *becoming* — of coming into that which is greater than it is. That which is in you is thus able to communicate with that which is in everything else.

The individual Life Force within is able to reach out beyond itself, even to the far reaches of the stars, but it does so by first going within itself. For it is within your own energy-system, at the centre of your being, that you are at one with both the visible and the invisible. So it is necessary to go within in order to reach the within of that which is without.

CHAPTER THREE

The Cosmos of the Shaman

IN BYGONE DAYS when shamans along with others in the tribe depended on their hunting skills to ensure that they and their families ate regularly, the art of working out ways of finding and catching their prey was called tracking and stalking. The hunter needed to know the whereabouts of the prey and be familiar with its movements and habits and likely stopping places, and to be able to get close enough to catch it.

Today we have no need to go hunting for food. Meat is attractively packaged and presented and far removed from any association with death. Provided we have the necessary cash, money in the bank, or credit card, we have only to reach for it on a supermarket shelf, load it onto a trolley, wheel it to a checkout point, and then take it home in the boot of a car. But the art of tracking and stalking is still necessary for us if our 'prey' is the acquisition of shamanic capabilities, which is far more elusive than the most cunning hunted animal.

Before 'civilization' overtook him, the native American would track and stalk his prey for some time – often for several hours, sometimes even for days – before deciding that he was in the best possible position to succeed in his quest. He would then carefully select from his quiver of arrows the one best suited to the conditions. Each was crafted and fashioned with meticulous care and with a particular task in mind; each was flighted to reach its objective swiftly and silently.

His bow would have been made from wood that had been matured and seasoned by time, like his mind, and was symbolic of the mind. The sinew bow-string was strung taut like his emotions. His hand represented the spirit directing the arrow to a precise spot on the target. The quiver, too, would have been crafted lovingly and with skill for as the protector and container of the hunter's resources it represented his body. The arrows represented the way life was lived as a result of the choices and decisions that were made – the acts of will and the thoughts.

That was the shaman/hunter's spiritual understanding of the bow and arrow and quiver. We need to carry that 'equipment' in our minds in the quest and pursuit of the 'prey' we are seeking, which is the kind we can use to nourish and enrich our individual lives, to satisfy our dreams and aspirations and fulfil our potentials.

To track down shamanic power – the ability to do shamanic work – we need to know the most likely places where it might be found. We must learn how to recognize it, and how to approach it so that it does not slip away. We need to know how to hold on to it when it is 'caught'. And, of course, as the shaman/hunter had to know how to cook his prey so that it could be eaten, so we need to understand how shamanic ability can be made part of ourselves, and its power put to beneficial use in our lives and those of others our lives touch.

If a hunter wanted to catch sight of his prey he had to be quiet and still, and these attributes are essential in the tracking of shamanic power. In what sort of environment are you likely to find signs of that power? Well, for a start, it is unlikely to be where there's lots of human activity. If you were to take a radio or cassette player into the woods or countryside and turn it on to maximum volume you would hardly expect any wild life to stick around! So it has to be a place where you can be quiet for a time, and where you are not going to be disturbed or distracted. Indoors, it means a room in the house or the apartment that is away from the activities of others, and where you can be confident of not having sudden demands on your attention. If that means taking the phone off the hook for half an hour or more, so be it. Ourdoors it means a quiet spot, and not a public park where there is a lot of human activity. It means a natural environment that is away from any hustle and bustle and where you can feel close to Nature. Such places become your power spots.

A power spot is a place which emits energy that has a beneficial effect on the person or persons there. Major power spots are sites that have been regarded as sacred because of their powerful influence on people using them. A personal power spot is a pocket of Earth energy whose frequency is in tune with your own energy field and will amplify it. So a personal power spot raises your frequency level and clarifies the mind so you feel inspired and energized.

EXERCISE 6: Establishing your personal power spot

Indoors: To perform any kind of shamanic work you need somewhere to feel comfortable, at ease and free from distractions and possible disturbances. Do bear in mind that some shamanic work transcends the limitations of time and space so you must find a place where you will be untroubled and be completely relaxed. Size and appearance are irrelevant. It is your Mind Space that is important, not the physical area, so if you have a spare room, an attic, basement, or even a workshop that can double up to provide you with this Mind Space and quiet time for your shamanic endeavours, all well and good. If not, a corner of a bedroom, or other space that is not going to be used by other members of the household for a time will do. You convert it into your personal power spot by simply switching the space on to shamanic work at the beginning of a session, and switching it back for ordinary mundane activity at the conclusion. I will explain how this can be done shortly.

So look around now for that space. Arrange it in such a way that there is somewhere to sit and a convenient working surface where you can write notes. Also there should be sufficient floor space for you to lie down on a blanket for some of the shamanic work.

Outdoors: Go and find an outdoor spot in Nature where you can relax without disturbance. A small clearing among a group of trees is ideal, but the precise setting is unimportant. You must feel perfectly comfortable there, and feel 'at one' with the surroundings.

If you live in a country area this should not present difficulties, and you may have several options. If so, visit each one and choose the place that feels right. If, however, you are in a big city your choice may be limited to a park or some other natural setting. Avoid any area where there is likely to be a lot of human activity. Most cities do have attractive parklands where it is possible to find a quiet spot near some trees where you can sit undisturbed for a while and establish a close link with Nature.

Get those two power spots established now.

Now back to our hunter. He would need to consider the times when his prey was most likely to appear – at dawn and dusk, perhaps – or when it was most abundant during the year. The same applies to discovering shamanic power. Your senses are more likely to attune to subtle energies at periods in the daily cycle when external activity is not at its height. Personally I find the early morning period, just before dawn and shortly after the sun has risen, to be the most productive for creative and meditative work. Indeed, much of my writing is done between 5am and 8am each day. Similarly, the time around dusk when twilight signals a closing down of Nature's external activities and the day's work is behind you, is another potentially suitable period. Again, it is what suits you that is the most important, and the best time for you personally is the period of the day when you feel under the least pressure.

On the yearly cycle, the days around the times of the eight seasonal festivals of the ancient peoples of the northern hemisphere are also potentially fruitful times to connect with the unseen forces. These ancient seasonal 'peaks' are described in some detail in *Earth Medicine*; but I will deal with them briefly here.

The Spring Equinox around 21 March, when day and night are equally balanced, was the ancient *Festival of Awakening*. It is a time when new life is springing forth from that which was once 'dead'.

Beltain (beginning of May) was the ancient *Festival of Expectation* when

Nature's energies were rising and coming into flower. It is a time for sharing, uniting, and for harmonization.

The Summer Solstice around 21 June, when daytime is at its longest, was the ancient *Festival of Attainment* when solar power is reaching its peak. It is therefore a time for culmination.

Lammas (beginning of August) was the ancient *Festival of Reminder* when Nature produces the first fruits of her endeavours.

The Autumn Equinox around 22 September, when daytime and night-time are equally balanced, was the ancient *Festival of Thanksgiving*. Its emphasis is on distribution and on the importance of both giving and receiving.

Samhain (beginning of November) was the ancient *Festival of Remembrance* when the seen and unseen, dream and reality, merged. It is a reminder that the visible and invisible, Light and Darkness, are co-equal partners in the Wheel of Life.

The Winter Solstice around 22 December, when night is longest, was Yuletide, the ancient *Festival of Rebirthing* when the seeds of potential begin to stir. It recognized the rebirth of Light and gave a reminder that with light there is also shadow, so light and darkness need to be seen as aspects of the same thing.

Finally, Imbolc around 2 February was the *Festival of Renewal*, an occasion for cleansing and purification in preparation for fresh approaches.

Totems, symbols, emblems, shamanic tools and implements, and shamanic maps like the Medicine Wheel, are all tracks or magikal paths that can lead us to our prey – to where shamanic power is manifested. Having located it, the next stage is to stalk it so that it can be caught and used. Let us consider stalking with regard to shamanic power.

When approaching his prey, the hunter kept out of sight, so as not to frighten it away. How did he ensure his 'invisibility'? Simply by becoming part of the environment – by camouflage. If you want to capture shamanic power you must learn to become part of the power environment; you have to become a participant with it, rather than an observer of it. So let me stress again: shamanism is a way of experienced knowledge. You have to *do* it to *know* it. It is more than an exercise of the intellect.

In order to blend in with his environment, the hunter had to be aware of, and adapt to, changes around him, and in stalking his prey he needed to assess its nature and habits as well as the pace at which it moved. So, too, we need to adjust our nature and habits to synchronize our vibrational rate with the power. This is the purpose of shamanic drumming. It temporarily modifies the rate of vibration of brain waves, enabling a gentle charge in awareness to take place so we can be aware of other levels of our Being. The drumming takes the consciousness out of

Time. It transfers this consciousness from the 'Tonal' region of material existence (which is conditioned by the measurement of time), to the 'Nagual' region (which is the stream of universal consciousness within the Life Force) which is a state of Timelessness. The drumming just are safely returns the consciousness from timelessness back into Time.

'Tonal' is a word derived from the language of the Aztec Indians. It refers to physical world existence and material reality. Everything is conditioned by time – that is, it manifests in a certain form for only a period, for only a measurement of time. In the Tonal the spirit ensouls or gives life to forms. As long as the form can be sustained there is life; but when the flow is interrupted or the form breaks down, then the organized higher expression of the Life Force in that form in that place and at that time, ceases. The individuality of the being, which thought of and created the form of the Life Force to ensoul, returns from whence it came – to the Nagual. Spirit cannot die, or 'God' dies. The Life Force and the Law come directly from the Great Spirit to us; our individualities are part of the Great Spirit, and use the Law and Life Force to express themselves materially. It is the Law of our Being. That is why we were made.

'Nagual' is a word also derived from the Aztec language, and means 'disguised' or 'masked'. It refers to a reality that lies behind the 'disguise' of matter – in other words, non-material reality. In the Nagual the individual being experiences eternity, which is a timeless 'now'.

So stalking has now brought us to a further realization – that it is not merely a matter of hunting and catching our 'prey' and making use of it as if it were something independent of ourselves. We have both to consume it and be ourselves modified by it. So let me recap: in order to 'catch' shamanic power you need to be in the right place at the right time, become part of the power environment, and then move with it.

In ancient times a tree was a symbol of the connection between the physical and temporal, and the spiritual and eternal. The Roman occupiers of ancient Britain sometimes referred to Celtic Druids as 'knowers of trees', because they were often observed apparently talking to trees and worshipping their gods in groves. Shamans of the northern traditions of Britain, Europe and Scandinavia, likened the Cosmos – the entirety of all existence – to a living tree, an evolving organism with intelligence and an awareness of its own being. So in our stalking of shamanic power we need to look at the symbolism of this Cosmic Tree. Nordic shamans called it 'the Tree of Yggdrasil'. Yggdrasil is a Nordic name meaning 'horse of Ygg', Ygg being a name for Odin, a Nordic shaman-deity who was regarded in mythology as the All-Father or 'Father' of All. Odin's horse was a mythological creature that could travel to other realms of existence. So the Tree of Yggdrasil was a symbol of access to Other-worlds – to other states of being.

The Cosmic Tree comprised different levels of existence and consciousness which were often referred to as 'worlds'. These contained zones or realms of reality. The levels can be related to various aspects of the mind: to normal waking consciousness, to the subconscious and unconscious, and to a higher state of consciousness which one might call the 'superconscious'.

Although it may be necessary to compartmentalize the mind in this way in an attempt to understand its function, it is important not to overlook the fact that the mind itself is a totality. So what is being considered, whether referring to the conscious, subconscious, unconscious or superconscious, is an aspect of the mind. The Cosmic Tree illustrated this holistic principle.

The manifested material world of waking consciousness was in the 'middle', and represented by the trunk of the Cosmic Tree. Above was a higher state of consciousness, portrayed by the branches lifting skywards. Below was a nether region of subconscious and unconscious activity, represented by the roots and by the soil around them. Water through the soil – the unconscious – surfaced in the Well of Wyrd, a well of destiny where past actions worked through Time to affect the Present and to influence the Future.

There was a horizontal as well as a vertical plane to the Cosmic Tree, for it was multi-dimensional and indicated that the Cosmic ecology was structured like a snowflake and could be represented by the simple symbol of a diagonal cross with a vertical line through its centre.

The snowflake symbol was a means of emphasizing the multi-dimensional reality of the encircled cross. It was a two-dimensional image to indicate that there was a central shaft or spindle and an 'above' and 'below', as well as four directions of left, right, forward and behind. So it could be regarded as sky above, earth beneath, west, east, north and south.

The concept of Light and Darkness also took on a rather profound meaning in the ancient northern tradition. Light above was indicated by Cosmic Fire – which was light at its maximum vibration – and Darkness beneath was indicated by Cosmic Ice, which was regarded as a 'solidification' of the dark energy. The union of the polarized forces of Fire and Ice, Light and Darkness, Yang and Yin, God and Goddess, was what produced the manifest universe 'in the middle'.

The shaman regarded all polarized forces in the universe as opposite ends of a union. So, faced with an expression of only one of these powers, he did not overlook its essential unity. Day and night, for instance, were not therefore regarded as separate phenomena but as different expressions of the same thing. What appeared as matter was a 'solid' manifestation of

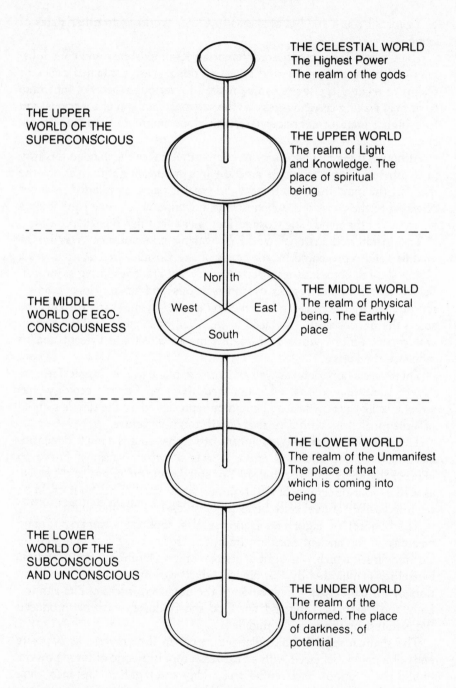

THE CELESTIAL WORLD
The Highest Power
The realm of the gods

THE UPPER
WORLD OF THE
SUPERCONSCIOUS

THE UPPER WORLD
The realm of Light
and Knowledge. The
place of spiritual
being

North

West   East

South

THE MIDDLE
WORLD OF EGO-
CONSCIOUSNESS

THE MIDDLE WORLD
The realm of physical
being. The Earthly
place

THE LOWER WORLD
The realm of the Unmanifest
The place of that
which is coming into
being

THE LOWER
WORLD OF THE
SUBCONSCIOUS
AND UNCONSCIOUS

THE UNDER WORLD
The realm of the
Unformed. The place
of darkness, of
potential

Fig 4. Levels of the Cosmic Tree of Yggdrasil

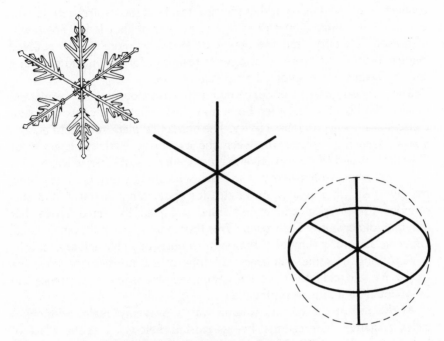

Fig 5. The snowflake symbol of multi-dimensional reality

that which was invisible spirit. Death was not regarded as a cessation of life but as an aspect of living – a laying aside of one form of existence and transition to another.

Manifestation into the realm of physical reality also took on two principal aspects – energy and matter – each of which was interchangeable. Energy contained the Cosmic pattern from which matter was shaped, and matter ultimately returned to the primal energy from which it was formed. The Universe was thus understood anciently as a conscious, living, organic and evolving Being, subject like everything else to the laws of its own existence – a law-abiding and law-enforcing organism. Humanity and other forms of life were seen as part of this 'whole'.

Unlike some Creation myths, the cosmos of the shaman was not regarded as having come into existence out of nothing. Instead it was seen as the manifestation of an orderly universe out of a primal substance that was already 'there', though in a state of chaos. In northern mythology the slaying of the giant Ymir, and the reshaping of his body, was an allegory intended to impart the knowledge that an ordered and evolving Universe was fashioned out of the living substance of the Cosmos. It was patterned like a snowflake and structured like a tree. The trunk or central axis connected the 'Middle' World of physical reality at the 'centre' with Other-worlds. 'Above' (the Upper World) were powers of knowledge, enlighten-ment and creativity, and the abode of 'gods' or more highly evolved beings. 'Below' (the Lower World) were realms of formation and gestation and the realms of less-evolved elemental beings.

The vertical pillar was concerned with consciousness of being and defined the bisection between Light and Dark – between conscious, sub-conscious and unconscious activity. The horizontal plane related to energy and showed the bisection between the expansive electrical energies of Cosmic Fire, and the constrictive magnetic energies of Cosmic Ice.

These Other-worlds were not so much separated by distance or by time, but by their vibrational wavelength, for they interpenetrated and sur-rounded the physical and material and occupied the same 'space' but different 'dimensions'. The Cosmic Tree thus embraced a multi-dimensional Universe and was a symbol of the essential unity of all life and at all levels.

According to some shamanic traditions of the northern peoples, the Upper, Middle and Lower 'worlds' comprised nine realms of existence and these could be indicated on the Tree of Yggdrasil.

At the top of the vertical column was a 'heavenly' realm, sometimes called Asgard, where celestial beings existed. Below it was the 'Place of Enlightenment' – the realm of the Mind, the Abode of Thought, and the fertile birthplace of Ideas. In the middle was the realm of material manifes-tation which was conditioned by Time, the Home of the personality self and of ego-consciousness. Below was a subterranean realm, related to subconscious activity, where shapes were formed from thought patterns. At the base of the column was a realm of inertia – the Place of Potential. It was sometimes referred to as *Hel* – a Germanic word meaning 'covering', because it covered the deepest areas of the unconscious. It had none of the associations attributed to the fiery 'Hell' of the myths of later religions.

On the horizontal plane were other aspects of being and of experience, which similarly formed part of the 'hidden' knowledge of the shamans.

The Runic shamans of the ancient northern peoples acquired much 'hidden' knowledge by the use of angular symbols (Runes) which could easily be carved on wood or chiselled into stone. Contrary to modern belief (based upon the conjecture of some anthropologists), Runes were not simply a secret code whose characters were used as substitutes for letters of the common alphabet. It is likely that the majority of Runic shamans could not read or write their own language, or Latin, which became the language of the scholar after the Roman influence. Runes actually repre-sented patterns of manifestation and the laws responsible for shaping forms into which energies could find expression. They were – and are – symbols of a Cosmic language, and are valid on all levels of existence.

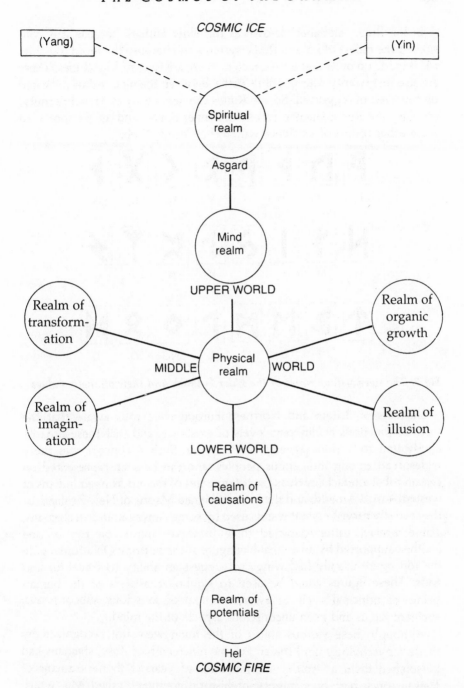

Fig 6. The nine realms or planes of existence positioned on the Tree of Yggdrasil

In the Runic 'alphabet', known as the Elder Futhark because it is considered the oldest of known Runic systems and because the word 'f-u-th-a-r-k' is made up of its first six characters, there are twenty-four Runes. There are also just twenty-four possible 'paths' between the nine realms indicated on the Tree of Yggdrasil. So the Runes can serve also as 'travel permits', enabling the Runic shaman to explore Inner Space, and as 'passports' to these other realms of existence within the Cosmic Web.

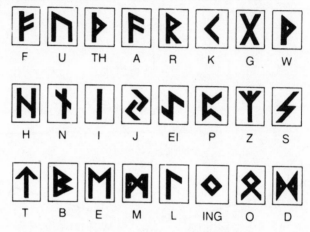

F   U   TH   A   R   K   G   W

H   N   I   J   EI   P   Z   S

T   B   E   M   L   ING   O   D

Fig 7. The twenty-four runes of the Elder Futhark and their phonetic values

Shamans of Britain and Northern Europe were thus aware that the Cosmos functions at different levels of existence, and that these broadly correspond to various aspects of the mind. Such a concept was fairly widespread among indigenous peoples, and can be seen represented on certain tribal artefacts, such as the totem poles of the red-skinned Indians of western North America and the brown-skinned Maoris of New Zealand, or the specially carved crystal wands used by some American Indian shamans. These artefacts often depicted three principal 'spirits' on top of one another, supported by an animal-like figure at the bottom. On a totem pole the top figure usually had wings to suggest an ability to travel far and wide. These figures could be used to symbolize aspects of the human being, of principal levels of awareness, and of conscious, subconscious, superconscious and even unconscious aspects of the mind.

Although these various states of the mind were not recognized by modern pyschology until the end of the nineteenth century, shamans had personified them as 'spirits' for hundreds of years. Kahuna shamans of Hawaii (once part of a mighty prehistoric continent called Mu, which disappeared under the Pacific Ocean during an ecological disaster when the Earth was pulled into a new and slightly longer orbit of the Sun) likened the subconscious to a 'hidden' spirit within the human entity which, although it was not able to talk, experienced emotion and secretly and silently served the consciousness of the individual to whom it was attached.

The inspirational and creative level of the mind which operated at a higher state of consciousness was recognized as the province of a 'higher spirit' – a 'High' Self – which was immortal and which motivated the individual towards spiritual aspirations and noble deeds. It was considered to guide and inspire the 'human' self, for it had divine-like qualities.

The Kahuna shamans considered these distinct 'spirit' intelligences or

Fig 8. A totem pole (left) with three figures or 'selves' supported by a base figure, and (right) a shaman's crystal wand which has representations of three 'spirits' carved in it

'selves' as a co-operating 'team'. We might regard them as various aspects of the total Self, operating in different ways but, like members of a sports' team who contribute their own skills and operate from individual positions, they function as a single unit and on different levels of consciousness.

Max Freedom Long, an American psychologist and religious historian who devoted much of his life to a study of the magician-priests of Hawaii and who wrote a number of books on his findings, referred to the personality that was involved in the conscious activities of everyday life, and which used the reasoning mind, as a 'Middle' Self. At another level was a 'Low' Self, which was concerned with memory, some activities of the subconscious mind and all those of the unconscious. Above these was a 'High' Self which operated at the level of the highest aspirations of the mind. Kahuna shamans regarded these 'selves' as 'personal' intelligences, or spirits, whose functions overlapped.

Among shamans of northern traditions, however, was an oral teaching that recognized a fourth intelligence — an instinctive and automative one which controlled and maintained the physical body, and which was responsible for its protection and survival. This intelligence operated at deep levels of unconscious activity, and was likened to an animal spirit because its actions seemed largely instinctive. Since it normally disappeared when the human being suffered death it was not regarded in the same way as the other 'spirits'.

Medicine Chief Silver Bear explained to me that these four intelligences are separated by intention. Each has its own particular function, and its own form of mental power; but each is only one aspect of the individual.

 The Cosmic Tree and the Medicine Wheel are all ancient shamanic maps which shamans of different cultures have used to understand these aspects of their individuality and to reach different levels of consciousness. Each technique has been effective within its own culture, but has derived from an earlier universal system of prehistory. By recognizing the parallels and integrating the principles into a single harmonic system in the spirit of the travelling shamans, I hope not only to get closer to the original system, but also to provide modern people with a clear path to the Cosmos of the shaman, thus securing a firm foundation from which Inner Space may be explored and the benefits shared.

Travelling shamans who went beyond the limitations of their own tribal customs recognized that no single group possessed all Truth, and so journeyed from tribe to tribe and place to place seeking knowledge, gaining new insights, weaving what they learned into what they already knew, and imparting wisdom.

Let us now consider the mind. The mind is very elusive because it is intangible. Dictionaries define it as the seat of consciousness, and of thoughts and emotions. Scientists, philosophers and theologians are not entirely in agreement about what the mind is, but they know that the mind is not the brain. The brain is a physical organ and centre of sensation contained within the skull, and might be regarded as a bio-computer which is used by the mind. It can be located and measured because it is physical; the mind cannot, since it is intangible and infinite. So whilst we may not yet fully understand what the mind is, we do know it exists.

In order to aid our understanding of the mind, we may classify the way it operates into four functional levels. Of course, it is not really divided into compartments, for the simple reason that it has no form. But to comprehend an abstract concept, our reason needs something to 'grip' onto. This is the prime purpose of such categorization, and of a shamanic map.

The aspect of the total mind with which we are most familiar is the *Conscious Mind*, for we use this constantly during our normal, everyday activities. The Conscious Mind is the seat of the intellect; it is what we 'reason' with to arrive at conclusions before determining our actions. We use it to interpret and make sense of the impressions we receive from the external environment. The Conscious Mind is the mind of 'self' we present to the world – the egotistical 'Human' Self, the 'Middle' Self, whose language is words and speech – the 'separate' or separated self.

The *Subconscious Mind* is that aspect of the mind that appears to act on instructions programmed into it by the Conscious Mind. These are the firm beliefs, attitudes and habits formed through early conditioning and by the environment, fears, phobias and complexes. It stores these along with a record of conscious happenings in its memory bank, and could be described as the 'servant' mind because it serves the Conscious Mind in this way. It is the mind of what I prefer to call the 'Hidden' Self because its activities are largely 'hidden' within; it communicates through imagery, symbols and feelings.

The *Unconscious Mind* is automative and operates unceasingly. From the moment of conception it works to build, maintain and repair the physical body, first according to instructions contained within the generic code, and later with those passed down from the subconscious. It is the mind of what I shall call the 'Body' Self because it operates at the very foundation level of the human body. Its language is impulsive – chemical and electrical.

The *Superconscious Mind* is the highest aspect of the total mind and has superior mental powers. It is the source of all the knowledge you might want or are ever likely to need. The Superconscious Mind brings knowledge into the consciousness through sudden flashes of illumination. It is the source of inspiration and creativity, and is the mind of the 'High' Self. Its language is telepathic.

The four aspects of the total mind thus relate to aspects of the total Self and exist simultaneously:

The *Human Self* is that aspect of the total Self that expresses itself through personality, and is concerned with making choices and decisions in practical, everyday living. It exercises reasoning ability and analyses, categorizes, makes judgements and comparisons, and forms beliefs and opinions.

The realm of the *Hidden Self* is subconscious, so its actions are 'beneath the surface'. It is conditioned by beliefs and attitudes imposed upon it, for it is a 'servant' self which responds to what it regards as 'authority'. In childhood, behaviour conditioning is largely through parents and teachers; in adolescence by social figures that are made objects of 'hero' worship; and in adulthood by the particular 'gods' to which the Human Self chooses to devote its time and energy. This subconscious 'self' has little reasoning power, but it does have memory. It learns physical skills through repetition and the voice of authority for it has a trusting nature and an inherent willingness to obey. It feels emotion, because the source of this is at a subconscious level. Emotion is a flow of energy stimulated by thought which, when experienced, can lead to action.

The *Body Self* is the biological intelligence of the body, and is its caretaker, protector and defender. It has an animalistic nature which is why it acts on instincts and impulses. It reacts to fear – which are emotions producing hormones, triggered by the Hidden Self – because it is primarily concerned with physical survival.

The *High Self* is our noblest 'self' whose emphasis is on principles and ethical values. The High Self has an over-view of one's life, for it can see into the past and the immediate future as well as the present. Thought patterns that are forming in the present, and from earlier actions, are seen in the process of becoming manifest. Answered prayer is a response of the High Self making changes to thought patterns, and of what is coming into physical being.

Kahuna shamans used a coded language through which ancient knowledge was communicated and kept intact. Words in Hawaiian – a Polynesian language which may be closest to that which was spoken in the 'lost' prehistoric continent of Mu – could be broken down into separate root words and combinations of syllables and vowels to uncover deeper meanings. The myths, legends, folk tales and sacred writings of various cultures similarly contained 'surface' meaning for general understanding and an inner, 'hidden' meaning which revealed deeper knowledge to those who were capable of receiving it. It should be understood that what was 'hidden' in this way was not necessarily intended to be a closely guarded secret for the benefit of a select few (though there may be justification for keeping certain knowledge from those who are likely to abuse it). It was merely hard to perceive because a certain state of spiritual development had to be reached before it could be readily understood.

Kahuna shamans knew the Human Self as *A-uhane* or *Uhane* – *Au* meaning spirit, self or the 'I', and *hane* meaning talk or talking. So *A-uhane* was the spirit that talks – the talking self. The Hidden subconscious Self was known as *A-unihipili* – *nihi* meaning young, hidden or silent; *pili* meaning clinging. So *A-unihipili* was the hidden and silent, child-like self that clings to the *A-uhane*. The High Self was known as *Aumakua* – *makua* meaning older, or parental. So *Aumakua* was the older and wiser self. Other shamans knew it as the *Hokkshidah*.

The High Self has been in existence for a very long time. It has both a male and female aspect, and its relationship with the Human Self is similar to that of loving parents towards a child. The High Self has formulated the individual's life plan so that it can thrive and develop through the schooling of life experiences obtained on the planet Earth. The common purpose of each human being is to 'evolve' towards something greater than it is. Mastering the challenges of human experience, and aligning the Human Self with the nobler purpose of the High Self, ensures that development.

When a neophyte in the ancient wisdom was being implored to 'Know Thyself', it implied far more than an understanding of the Human Self. It was stressing the needs to comprehend all aspects of being human, and to harmonize the different 'selves' into an integrated working partnership that would bring about a fulfilment of the true purpose of life – the soul's purpose – which was the reason for incarnating at a particular time and place. This is so today, and lies at the heart of shamanism.

In order to communicate, the Human Self uses words. These are an expression of the energy of our thoughts and ideas, and through the use of words we can convey these to other human beings. The Hidden Self does not use words, but communicates via images and feelings. The High Self also employs imagery and intuitive promptings, and flashes of inspiration. The Body Self's mode of communication is electro-chemical impulses. Images, intuitive feelings, inspirational ideas and impulses are all energy forms used by these different aspects of the total Self and of the total Mind. Everything in existence is also made up of energy forms, arranged in continually changing combinations. So the 'language' of imagery and impulses make communication possible with the energy-patterns of other life forms – with other 'intelligences' or 'spirits' – and between different levels of existence on Earth and in the Universe. We are each endowed

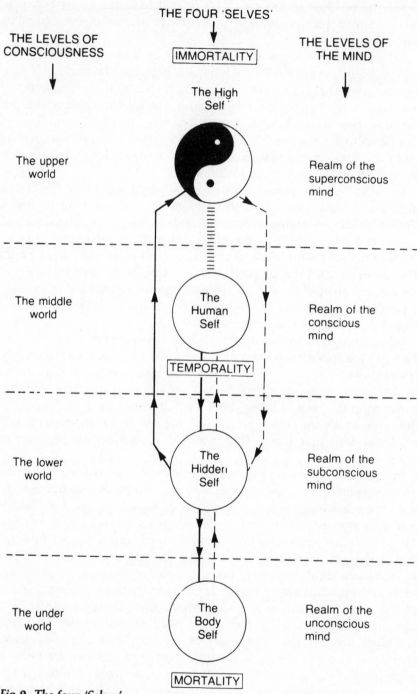

THE FOUR 'SELVES'

THE LEVELS OF
CONSCIOUSNESS

IMMORTALITY

THE LEVELS OF
THE MIND

The High
Self

The upper
world

Realm of the
superconscious
mind

The middle
world

The
Human
Self

Realm of the
conscious
mind

TEMPORALITY

The lower
world

The
Hidden
Self

Realm of the
subconscious
mind

The under
world

The
Body
Self

Realm of the
unconscious
mind

MORTALITY

Fig 9. The four 'Selves'

with the 'equipment' to make this possible. However, through ignorance of its existence and of how to operate it or even recognize it, it remains dormant. Shamanic power provides an ability to put that 'equipment' to use.

Through an awareness of these 'selves' and aspects of the mind and of the realms of consciousness, the shamanic adventurer is not only able to explore the Cosmos itself and to pass from one level of reality to another, but also to have greater command of his or her own personal life in the 'Middle' World of physical existence.

Our personal environment in this 'Middle' World is a manifestation of thought patterns – both individual and collective – and contains reflections and representations of our own thoughts, beliefs, attitudes, fears and complexes. The physical body is a materialized thought of the 'parental' High Self who 'fashioned' it. The personal world which contains the totality of experience has – to a large extent – been fashioned by thoughts, fears, phobias and inhibitions of the conscious mind. These have been impressed into the subconscious which, by its very nature, then seeks to find ways of bringing them into realization. This also applies collectively, which affects our own personal world as well. In other words, we each to an extent create our own reality, as individuals, as families, as communities, and as nations and races.

If we genuinely want to change the outside world and make it a better place, we must first change ourselves on the 'inside'. How can we begin to do this? An admonishment of American Indian shamans is never to take life too seriously, and the triggering device for that inner change is simply a smile. Indeed, Taoist masters taught that the secret of establishing harmony with yourself was to smile. So learn to smile! It does more than make you feel good: a smile has tremendous power. It transmits energy which has a harmonizing effect, and that energy is Love-energy.

Love-energy is a power that brought everything into existence, and from which everything is derived. The Elements of Fire, Air, Water and Earth stem from it. The whole of Creation quite literally was brought about by the power of Love. This Love-energy should not be confused with sex-energy, though this can be a positive expression of it. In shamanic understanding, love is an unconditional sharing of the experience of life – of the Life Force – and desires only the harmonious growth and development of whatever it is directed towards. In a human being this Love-energy arouses feelings of joy and happiness in both the receiver and the giver because it actually produces a secretion that nourishes not only the physical body but the entire being. This is why when you smile at someone they'll smile back – an immediate response to a warm feeling inside that someone desires their well-being. In an instant Love-energy has been given out and returned, and the atmosphere transformed. So if you can learn to smile at yourself you can bask in a warm, harmonizing energy that will penetrate your whole being and permeate your entire energy-system. How can you learn to smile at yourself? By developing an inward smile. Try this simple exercise that, if performed regularly, can quite literally transform your attitude to life.

EXERCISE 7:   The inward smile

Sit comfortably with the back erect and the feet firmly in contact with the floor. Close your eyes to screen out any external distractions. Relax the mouth and allow it to form into a smile. Now you are going to turn that smile inward, and into yourself – into your Hidden Self.

Direct that smile into your eyes. It is not a matter of attempting to create a visual image of the eyes in your mind, but rather of moving your awareness into your eyes. So put your attention into your eyes, and imagine that smile shining out to absorb everything in its harmonizing energy. Then switch your attention to your face and jaws. Imagine the warm glow of your smile smoothing out any wrinkles in your face and releasing any tension in your jaws. Then move your awareness to the throat and neck, and concentrate your smile on that part of your body. Next, turn your attention to your chest and lungs and smile on them, too. Then let your heart bask in your smile, and with every heart-beat feel it pumping Love-energy to every cell in your being. Move your attention then to the abdomen. Smile on your liver and smile on your kidneys. Now to the base of the spine; move your attention slowly up the spine and into the head, smiling as you go. Finally, move down to the navel, where a central control centre is located just beneath the surface. It is the point from which you were first knitted together as a human being. It is the point at which you are connected with the Cosmic Web, and with everything else in existence. So smile into your navel.

Your whole being should now feel aglow. You have a pleasant sensation of well-being – not only of being healthy, but that all is well with the world. That is the transforming power of the inward smile!

Open your eyes, but retain that smile.

Practise this inward smile first thing in the morning and last thing at night. Perform it several times during the day. It can be done almost anywhere – on a bus or train, in the car on the way to and from work, and during meal breaks and quiet times. Best of all, perform it before facing any problematical, difficult or traumatic situation. Your Hidden Self will respond positively.

ENERGIZING POWER

Our tracking and stalking has shown us that in order to capture shamanic power we need to start from a suitable place, our timing has to be right, we require a map to help us find our way, and directing intelligence to locate it and put it to use. We have experienced a glimpse of harmonizing power. Now we need to understand more about the energizing forces that are the very essence of life itself.

The Cosmic Tree revealed that the various zones of reality are connected by a central shaft – the trunk. Now this is more than just a supporting pillar; it is a channel through which sap flows, containing the vital energies of the tree. Since this is the Cosmic Tree, it must be energized by forces that are the very essence of life itself. These could be likened to breath, for they are the forces that keep things alive.

Kahuna shamans, and some American Indians, referred to vital life force as *mana* (pronounced 'mah-nah'). Taoists of the East called it *chi* (pronounced 'chee'), and the Zen monks of Japan referred to it as *ki* ('kee'). Yogis, and mystics of the West have used the Sanskrit word *prana* ('prahna') to name vital spiritual energy that comes in with the breath, and shamans of northern peoples used a Norse word *megin*. These words of different languages have similar meaning – 'breath' or 'spirit energy'. They imply an invisible, fluid force that can be taken in with the breath. Indeed, it might be likened to life-giving fluid such as very fine rain, which causes seeds to grow and come to fruition. Or its fluidity might be likened to an electrical current which can operate at different strengths. The faster the body to which the energy is directed vibrates, the higher the quality of the vital force needed to empower it.

The vital force necessary for shamanic work is essentially the same as that which is required for our physical and Energy Bodies. The fundamental difference is that it is consciously controlled and its supply is wilfully increased, and this can be achieved through a special kind of rhythmic breathing called the Shamanic Breath. This activates the power centres of the Energy Body which distribute this vital force to all levels of our being. A sign of an increased flow of this electric-like energy within the physical body is a warm, slightly tingling sensation in the palms of the hands and at the fingertips. Experience it for yourself.

EXERCISE 8: The shamanic breath

Go to your indoor power spot where you can be undisturbed and relaxed for a few minutes. Take off your shoes and sit comfortably with the back erect, legs uncrossed, and the feet firmly on the floor. Clasp the palms together lightly, with the right palm over the left, and resting on your lap.

Close your eyes and breathe in slowly through the nostrils, pushing the abdomen out to enable air to enter the deeper recesses of the lungs. Continue to breathe in for a count of three seconds, and imagine that you are drawing in tiny globules of golden light with the breath. Then hold the breath to a count of three seconds. Don't strain in any way; you must feel comfortable at all times. During the 'holding' the cosmic light is being absorbed into the chakra power centres. Exhale gently through the mouth to a count of four seconds, pulling in the abdominal muscles as you do so.

As you inhale, 'suck' in the 'ma' part of the word 'mana', stretching it out to the full in-breath – *mmma-aaaahh*. Pause to a count of three seconds, then as you expel the air from your lungs vibrate the 'na' part of the word – *nnnna-aaaahh* – stretching it out to the full four-second count of the out-breath. Then pause for a count of four seconds before repeating the sequence.

The word 'mana' is not just a name for vital spirit-energy. It is also a word of power. It is a word found in the Hawaiian language, though it originates from an earlier civilization. It means 'to empower'. 'Ma' is the active Yang portion of the word and 'na' is the quiescent Yin element.

This sequence of *receive – hold – release – pause* to a count of 3–3–4–4 is a rhythm of the creative and formative forces of the Universe. Shamanically, 'three' indicates 'the everything', for qualitively the number is made up of the union of the masculine and the feminine (1 + 2 = 3). Four is also a sacred number and qualitively expresses duality paired and in balance (2 × 2 = 4). So 'four' is the power of balance, alignment and harmony. The sequential rhythm of the Shamanic Breath thus takes on profound meaning.

It may take a little practice to get the hang of this Shamanic Breath technique, but once you have established the rhythm continue the exercise for three or four minutes. You are likely to experience a warm sensation in the palms of the hands as if you are holding a small but invisible ball, and a feeling of elation. This is a clear indication that the vital energy has been generated. Complete the exercise by taking a long, deep breath and having a good stretch. Stretch your arms and your legs slowly as you might after a good night's sleep, and gradually allow your breathing to return to its normal pace.

This shamanic breathing technique and the deliberate taking in of vital energy is a preliminary to shamanic journeying which I shall explain in detail in Chapter 7, and it is an essential preliminary of shamanic work. Like electricity, this vital force can be consciously directed or transferred from one place to another. The shaman uses rhythmic breathing, visualization, and sound – drumming, rattling, chanting, singing and words of power – to increase the supply and also to raise or regulate its quality.

We have now not only tracked and stalked shamanic power, but have also actually captured and absorbed it into ourselves and have been absorbed by it, for in it we live and move and have our being. In this chapter you have experienced knowledge that has eluded some of the world's most learned men throughout the ages, but which has been part of the wisdom of shamans for many thousands of years!

CHAPTER FOUR

The Shaman's Web of Power

AS WE HAVE SEEN, a shamanist's view of the Cosmos is different from the materialistic one in which everything in the world around us is perceived as being separate from and independent of everything else. Shamanists live in an intricate and infinite Web in which everything is connected by strands of energy, like the arteries and capillaries that carry the life blood to every cell of the body.

Within the Web we are each tracing our own path and shaping our own reality, not only by what we do, but by our very thoughts which condition our attitudes, and the use to which we put our energies. And since we are connected to everything and everyone else in the Web by fibre-like energy streams, we affect and influence other participants – human and non-human – who are equally part of the Web. We are full of space, located in an organized energy-system within the force-form matrix which is our expression. We ourselves are a web, connected to all other webs within the Greater Web of which we are a part.

This concept of the Web is used by shamans as an explanation of the connected wholeness and completeness of all that is in existence – without beginning or ending, all linked together, and each evolving within the Law of its own being.

The Web thus has reality and was the basis of the circular philosophy of the American Indian and North European and other peoples. It has specific uses as part of the inner resources of the shaman. These inner resources constitute a shamanist's 'medicine' – his knowledge and power. He knows that the Cosmic Web links all the 'circles' of existence from the lowest to the highest, threading through and interconnecting all levels, and joining the Past and the Future with the Present. Whereas the Cosmic Tree and the Medicine Wheel can be regarded as maps for the Conscious Mind, the Cosmic Web can be seen as a chart for all levels of Mind, though it is through the subconscious that the shaman is enabled to make connections with anything and anyone else. A shamanist's consciousness can be considered to act like the spider which is connected with every part of the web through the fine energy stands that constitute it.

Whilst the Cosmic Tree and the Medicine Wheel are analytical devices

Fig 10. The Yin and Yang mandala

which the human mind has produced after studying Earth energies and their behaviour, and to help the shaman feel his way about the Cosmos, the Cosmic Web is the reality within which all exists – Tree, Wheel, shaman, all.

Common to American Indians and the ancient northern peoples was a recognition that the Cosmos was maintained in existence through the interaction of two great polarities that are inherent in the expression of all things. The active, conceptual, masculine principle, the Source of Light and Energy, was personified by American Indians as the spiritual Sun or Father Sky 'above'. Some cultures called it 'Father' God, and still do. The complementary polarity was the formative, nurturing, feminine principle, the 'Mother' of Life, personified as an Earth mother 'beneath', or by some cultures as the 'Goddess'.

Eastern Taoists expressed these twin Powers in the Yin and Yang mandala. Out of the Ultimate Reality – represented by the circle – came these dual Powers, represented by black and white dolphin-like figures, the black being the feminine and the white the masculine. These actual Powers were represented as constantly striving for union whilst at the same time being 'opposed' to one another, thus establishing the Law of Constant Change which is evident throughout all manifestation.

The black figure has a white dot within it and the white figure a black dot, illustrating that each contains within it the seed of its opposite, thus establishing the principle of the development of the essence or spirit of all things.

Although this symbol is of Eastern origin, its concept was shared and understood by other cultures and especially so by American Indians and the Eurasian peoples.

Shamans are aware that the source of every entity – whether human, animal, plant, mineral or celestial – is its spirit. Spirit is the individuated Life Force that exists within all forms but is 'hidden' because it is non-physical. The shaman cultivates a direct link with the spirits of living things through his own spirit. The spirit is the invisible essence of whatever is manifested – the power that is within every form and which determines its own uniqueness. But spirit is 'hidden' behind physical 'appearance'. The physical is what *appears*; the spirit is what *is*. So elusive is spirit that it is beyond the power of the intellect to adequately comprehend it. It can only be spiritually discerned.

Spirit is contained within every energy-system and is, in fact, the conscious intelligence.of the being formed by that energy-system. It is that which directs the energy and causes it to form patterns under the law of its own being, depending on how it 'organizes' itself to experience expression and to evolve. When a shamanist communicates with the spirit of a tree or a stone, animal or bird, he is in touch with its energy-source, the source of its being and its existence.

Because shamanists can communicate with spirits they are sometimes compared with spiritualist mediums. Shamanists, however, are not mediums. They do not give their power to external spirits however benevolent they may seem to be. Whereas a medium is rarely aware of what is said or what is happening during a period of deep trance, a shamanist is fully alert and in control of his or her own freewill all through a shamanic experience.

The ability to do shamanic work does not, therefore, come from some outside source: it exists already. It is within. It is only a matter of harmonizing one's own spirit energy with natural forces that are in the Universe, and making wilful use of them. Intention is what determines how the energy is to be used and directed. And intention is of the very essence, for energy operates in accordance with Cosmic Law, under which all energy returns ultimately to its Source. This is why intention must be motivated by Love. Love harms none and has beneficial effects. Harmful intent rebounds ultimately on the one who instigated it and is therefore self-destructive. It acts against the evolutionary growth of the individual in every aspect of being – physical, emotional, mental and spiritual.

If you want to do shamanic work, the power centres of your own energy-system must be awakened and developed. They activate the inner senses – the three inner ears and the eight inner eyes – that have been mostly dormant through lack of use. The power centres, as you have already experienced, draw in vital force from the cosmic reservoir in which we live and move and have our being.

When you perform shamanic breathing (as in Exercise 8), you increase the supply of vital cosmic force into your energy-system. This character-ized energy is drawn in from the cosmic reservoir with the breath, much as a fish extracts oxygen from the water in which it is immersed. It is distributed to the physical and subtle bodies of the energy-system through power centres which are saucer-like etheric 'organs', usually referred to as 'chakras'. This is a Sanskrit word which means 'whorling vortex' or 'wheel'. The chakras are not located in the physical body but in the energy field that surrounds and interpenetrates it. They are responsible for absorbing the vital force, processing its energy, and distributing it to the physical body via the nervous and endocrine systems.

Eight main power centres are arranged in an octave in accordance with the universal Law of Harmonics – the structure of cycles of eight – and are located vertically and roughly in line with the spine. Each governs a particular function of the human entity. There are two others, one located beneath the feet and the other between the ankles.

Each power centre can be represented in the form of a flower with the number of petals indicating the frequency at which it functions compared to others. The greater the number of 'petals', the higher the frequency range and the finer the energy-flow. The power centres open up like the petals of a flower and reflect the degree of an individual's development. The 'higher' chakras unfold in proportion to spiritual growth, and as they become more active so an expansion in the person's consciousness takes place and the individual develops insight into non-physical realms.

Five of the ten major power centres are above the diaphragm, and five are below. These centres and their principal function are as follows:

BELOW THE DIAPHRAGM

Power centre 1: The Root chakra beneath the feet allows you both to draw energy up from the Earth, and to put energy into the Earth. It also 'grounds' or 'roots' you.

Power centre 2: The Feet chakra between the ankles is related to movement and balance and equilibrium.

Power centre 3: The Base chakra at the bottom of the spine connects to the motor nerves and is concerned with survival and protection. It reacts to stress.

Power centre 4: The Sacral chakra is concerned with motivation and with sexuality.

Power centre 5: The Solar Plexus chakra is a complex, multi-functional network centre. Part of its function is related to growth and development.

ABOVE THE DIAPHRAGM

Power centre 6: The Heart chakra is the centre of compassionate action and desires. It works on love.

Power centre 7: The Throat chakra is the communications centre and the link with 'inner' voices.

Power centre 8: The Base-of-the-Brain chakra is concerned with actions. The physical body is governed through it.

Power centre 9: The Brow chakra is the 'psychic' command post and centre of mental power.

Power centre 10: The Crown chakra is concerned with 'knowing' and links with the High Self – the highest aspect of your total being.

These power centres process and distribute the vital energy to the physical body through the endocrine glands and the sympathetic and parasympathetic nervous systems. This latter nervous system is a sophisticated network which conveys impulses of energy by electro-chemical means and which reacts to stimuli received from the physical senses. It operates the 'motor' functions of the body. The endocrine glands are groups of cells which secrete hormones, chemical 'messengers' that operate and control many of the functions of other cells and bodily tissues. The condition of these chakra power centres, therefore, affects the individual's health; indeed, many conditions of physical ill-health may be due to chakra imbalance and malfunctioning.

The power centres are also related to the individual's emotional and mental well-being and spiritual development, and indicate the quality of his life as an holistic entity. Fear, anxiety and stress, for instance, disturb the dynamic balance of these centres. Emotional traumas can impair the flow of energies through the chakras and result in erratic endocrine gland functioning and consequent imbalance of hormone activity. These centres can be greatly opened up and stimulated into flowing harmoniously through meditation and shamanic breathing. They are described in some detail in my book *The Medicine Way*.

Thoughts, normally rushing through the mind, are slowed down and even stilled in a meditative state. The mind is then relaxed and can be brought under control, and visualization becomes a powerful means of concentrating and directing thought. Thoughts are not just an activity of the brain. They are energy-patterns and can be the blueprints or moulds for what may by actualized into a condition or form that may be comprehended and experienced or seen. What we think we see externally in physical existence is not actually seen by the physical eyes at all; our eyes convey only impulses from light stimuli to the brain. The 'seeing' of these external images is actually done in the mind. Visualization is picturing in the mind in accordance with the will. The purpose of visualization shamanically is to trigger an immediate response from the subconscious aspect of the mind, to activate each chakra power centre in turn and to stimulate the entire energy-system with an intake of cosmic energy.

EXERCISE 9:   Energizing your power centres

Go to your indoor power spot and ensure that you won't be disturbed for at least half an hour or so. Take off your shoes, loosen your clothing, and sit comfortably so your feet are in contact with the floor.

Close your eyes and try to picture in your mind's eye a ball of white light, glowing like a white sun. Now visualize that sphere of light hovering just above your head. Let it rest there for a few moments then imagine it descending to rest on top of your head where your Crown chakra is located.

Now take a long, slow, deep breath. Feel your whole energy-system drawing in energy from that light. Breathe in the power of light. Energize yourself with enlightenment.

When you breathe out do so in a way that will not expel the light. So control the out-breath – just let the breath trickle gently from your mouth very, very slowly. In this way you will not be letting go of the light you have drawn in, only that which is not 'of' the light.

Perform this inbreathing and outbreathing several times, then visualize the ball of light moving down to your brow area where your Brow chakra is located. Take a deep breath and consider the illumination that the light is bringing to your mind, so that you may act with the clarity of a knowledge that comes from within. Repeat the inbreathing and outbreathing several times.

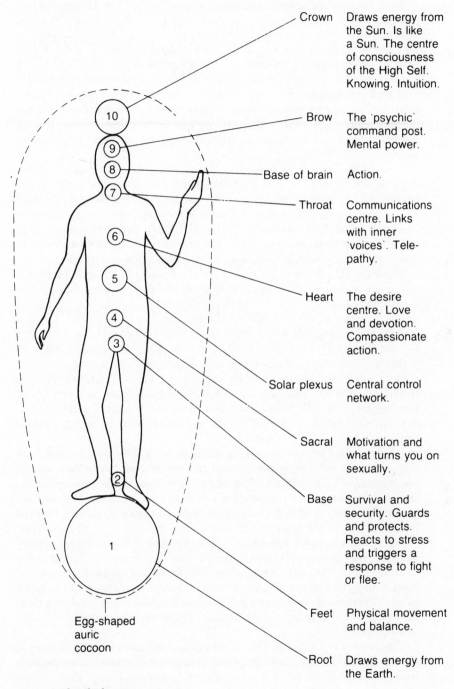

Crown   Draws energy from the Sun. Is like a Sun. The centre of consciousness of the High Self. Knowing. Intuition.

Brow   The 'psychic' command post. Mental power.

Base of brain   Action.

Throat   Communications centre. Links with inner 'voices'. Telepathy.

Heart   The desire centre. Love and devotion. Compassionate action.

Solar plexus   Central control network.

Sacral   Motivation and what turns you on sexually.

Base   Survival and security. Guards and protects. Reacts to stress and triggers a response to fight or flee.

Feet   Physical movement and balance.

Root   Draws energy from the Earth.

Egg-shaped auric cocoon

Fig 11. The chakra power centres

Now visualize the sphere descending to your throat. The Throat chakra is associated with communication, so after inhaling the light breathe out and visualize waves of light emanating from you, like ripples of water in a pond. As you take in more breaths regard the globe of light as a broadcasting station sending out and drawing in messages and information.

Next visualize the light moving down to your chest where the Heart chakra is located. As you take in a deep breath, think of it as a glowing ball of Love – Love whose warmth you can feel. As you breathe in and out a few times imagine sending out warm, embracing energies to the entire universe. It is the power of Love and Compassion, the greatest force for good in the entire Cosmos.

Now let the light move down to your solar plexus area and as you take a deep breath, visualize your energy-field lighting up all around you. As you breathe out feel the light energy expanding in all directions. Keep this up for a few minutes, before allowing the ball of light to move down to your abdomen where the Sacral chakra is located. The Sacral chakra is related to your sexuality and with what motivates you. So as you breathe in the light be aware of its great energizing power; as you breathe out feel its great driving force.

Move the light down to the base of the spine where the chakra's function is to provide energy which you can use to guard and protect yourself physically. Breathe in and out slowly and imagine the light encircling you like a protective shield. Generate a feeling of safety and security.

After performing this a few times, let the ball of light descend to a place between the ankles. Breathe in deeply and sense the thrill of your freedom of movement and balance. Imagine yourself dancing freely or skating on ice.

Now move the light down to just beneath your feet. Visualize it as a big beach ball, which is embedded into the Earth so you are safe and secure standing on it. Breathe in and out a few times and imagine the ball sending down roots of lights into the Earth itself, and you drawing up energy from the Earth.

Finally, as you breathe in imagine the light being drawn up through your legs and body and jetting out through the top of your head. Then, as you breathe out, feel the light cascading all around you like water from a fountain and soaking down into the ground beneath your feet. Breathe in to draw light upwards and out to let it flow down through your aura. Repeat this several times and your whole body will be aglow.

Before concluding this exercise, a further beneficial effect can be obtained by balancing the power centres you have activated. The symbol of balance is the encircled cross. The circle characterizes completion and containment, and the equal-armed cross represents the powers of Force and Form held in perfect balance. Energy follows thought, and so visualizing the encircled cross around each power centre to ensure the chakra is in perfect balance will have the desired effect.

This symbol can be created by using an imagined beam of light. Starting at the top ('north') draw a circle of light in a clockwise direction. When the light returns to the 'north' point, trace a vertical line down to the 'south'. Then follow the circle anti-clockwise to the 'east' point, continue it horizontally

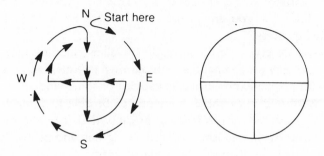

Fig 12. The visualized encircled cross

across the circle to the 'west', and from there follow the circle anti-clockwise until the light joins the 'north' point again.

Imagine drawing an encircled cross of light on the Crown of your head, then do the same at the Brow, the Base-of-the-Brain, the Throat, and then the Heart. Moving your consciousness down below the diaphragm, trace an encircled cross of light around your Solar Plexus, then the Sacral area, the Base of the Spine, between your ankles, and then beneath the feet.

The final stage of this exercise is to visualize a long black cloak that reaches right down to your feet. Wrap it around you and pull up the hood. Stay relaxed for a few moments then take a deep breath, get up from your seat, and have a good stretch.

What you have been doing in this exercise is to draw the light of consciousness into each of the main power centres in turn and flood your aura with light. In so doing you have stimulated your entire being. Wrapping a dark cloak around yourself in your imagination prevents this light energy from seeping away.

This exercise should be repeated daily if possible. If you have audio-recording equipment it would help to dictate this entire exercise onto a cassette tape, leaving pauses of two or three minutes between each stage to allow time for a number of inbreathings and outbreathings. You can then wear a headset and perform the exercise in a fully relaxed manner, without having to remember what comes next.

Once you have worked on your chakras in this way for a few days your insight – your inner 'seeing' – and your inner hearing will develop. You will have more frequent hunches about various situations as you become more intuitive and sensitive to the needs of others. You are likely also to become aware of being drawn to certain gemstones, to particular trees, and having a regard for animal species that you did not experience before. You may also find that you are being turned to for advice and help from unexpected quarters.

In today's society we are constantly travelling, moving into locations which are not always compatible with our own energies, and coming into contact with people experiencing negativity of some kind and who affect the way we are. It is essential, therefore, to be able to protect our own auras from unwanted, disruptive, and possibly destructive intrusions that may arise from such contacts. You can strengthen and protect your aura quickly and easily by the use of a simple shamanic visualization technique. The power of your own thought can put an invisible protective shield around you.

The following exercise should be performed each morning before you become involved with the chores and cares of the day, and at other times when you are knowingly about to enter an adverse situation. It strengthens the membrane of the aura, and encircles you with a protective shell. Any harmful external influence or thoughts – which are, in fact, energy-patterns – will simply bounce off or be diffused by this screen. It can be likened to the 'shield' of the Earth's atmosphere, which protects the Earth's surface and inhabitants.

EXERCISE 10:   Strengthening and protecting your aura

Sit comfortably with the palms of the hands resting on the knees. Close your eyes and relax by expelling air from the lungs, imagining that all tiredness and tension is draining out through your legs and into the ground beneath your feet.

Take a deep breath by pushing out the abdomen to a count of three seconds, then hold the breath to a count of three. Expel the air by pulling in the abdomen to a count of four, and then pause for another four seconds before repeating the cycle. This 3–3–4–4 rhythmic breathing cycle not only calms the mind and relaxes the body but invigorates the energy-system through ensuring a supply of vitalized energy.

Remember that the air around you contains not only the oxygen required to keep the body nourished and alive, but also the life essence which sustains your entire energy-system. As you breathe in visualize energy coming from the Earth and along the surface of the front of your body to the abdomen, then the chest, neck, head, and to just above your head. Suspend the bio-energy there as you hold the breath, then as the air is gently expelled imagine that energy flowing down your back to your legs and feet and back into the ground. As you pause for four seconds before repeating the cycle, visualize it resting there like a pool of still, clear water.

Continue this exercise for a few minutes until you feel invigorated. Then picture the aura around you like a warm glow. Imagine this atmosphere extending above your head, around your body, and below your feet, like a huge egg. Visualize a covering on the outside of the auric cocoon like a clear, plastic skin, which acts as a proctective shell.

Now, each time you breathe out direct the vital 'mana' energy which you have been building up to that auric skin. Imagine you are breathing into it and that as you do so it is changing from a thin, translucent membrane into a thick transparent shell – like bullet-proof glass – through which everything can be seen clearly, but which will shield you from any projectile or adverse influence. After a few more breaths just 'tell' the aura it is sealed and safe. Say aloud or mentally: 'Aura seal.' The aura will then be shielded and complete.

As we go about our daily lives, dust and grime from the atmosphere adheres to our physical bodies, and for our own health and comfort we need to wash it off. Our auras are similarly affected by our location and by the energy-fields of other humans, but it is 'psychic' substance which attaches to the aura, in the same way as cigarette smoke penetrates a fabric and 'sticks' to it.

American Indians had a special way of cleansing the aura. They used smoke from burning herbs which penetrated the aura and gently and effectively diluted and dispersed psychic 'dirt'. This method was called 'smudging' (see Chapter 5).

The herb they used is sage, which Indian tribes regard as a sacred plant whose special qualities set it apart for cleansing. The smoke from burning sage banishes negative energies from the surrounding atmosphere that are clinging to the aura. The smoke from dried sweetgrass, another North American sacred plant, has qualities that refresh the aura. One might liken it to the effect an after-shave lotion or a deodorant spray has on the physical body. Yellow bedstraw (*Galium verum*), a herb which grows in Britain and Northern Europe as well as North America, has similar virtues. Dried lavender can also be used. You can make your own smudge bundle by wrapping dried yellow bedstraw, and a few spikes of lavender and some sage leaves together with cotton thread.

The Indians made up a small, tight bundle of herbs, which was set alight until it smouldered, and the smoke was directed by vigorous movements of a feather fan. A smudge 'mix' can be used instead. Pour the contents of a couple of sachets of dried sage (or two heaped desertspoonsfuls) into a small fireproof bowl or metal dish, and sprinkle on a little dried lavender. You then just need matches or a lighter, and something with which to fan the smoke – a small piece of card will do. Later you will want to acquire a proper fan of feathers.

EXERCISE 11: Cleansing the aura

Light the mixture so that it is smouldering well. Hold the bowl or bundle in your left hand then fan the smoke with a piece of card or a feather fan held in the other hand. Fan it first towards your chest area (your Heart chakra), then upwards towards your throat and face and up over your head. Take a few good breaths as you do so, drawing the smoke into your lungs. The aroma is pleasant and the smoke is refreshing. Then fan the smoke down to your lower body and towards the feet. Repeat this process four times.

To smudge the atmosphere around you, simply fan the smoke away from you, turning yourself clockwise so that the smoke is fanned in all directions, and then finally above your head and down towards your feet.

Smudging should precede all shamanic work. It is as important as washing your hands before a meal, or taking a bath or shower. 'Grooming' the aura regularly in this way will be highly beneficial and will have a noticeable effect on the way you feel. It also ensures that the atmosphere around you is conducive to shamanic work.

Whenever you have been engaged in any kind of shamanic or meditative work, and especially when you have been trying to change the level of consciousness and linking yourself to different energy frequencies, it is essential that you 'earth' yourself afterwards so that your entire energy-system is aligned again for normal, everyday physical activity. If you do not do this thoroughly it is possible that any excess energy that has been generated may leave you with a feeling of being 'spaced out' and disoriented for a while. It also ensures that no excess energy is left in the atmosphere to affect other people, who might move into that space before the energy is dispersed. Such a practice is in accord with an important American Indian principle: Indians always left a place as they found it. They did this so efficiently that frequently it was difficult to tell that people had actually been there. So 'earth' yourself by performing the following simple exercise after each shamanic activity.

EXERCISE 12: 'Earthing' yourself

The simplest way to 'earth' yourself is just to flop in a heap on the ground or floor. Have the palms down, touching the floor, and just relax and feel 'grounded'. Visualize any excess energy draining from your hands and feet and being absorbed into the Earth to be returned to the Source. After a few seconds, take a deep breath and stretch your arms and legs. Breathe in again, and exhale and s-t-r-e-t-c-h. One more time – breathe in, exhale and s-t-r-e-t-ch.

Stand up and be aware of your physical body. Imagine the power centre beneath your feet rooting you to the ground. Breathe in and visualize drawing up energy from the ground through those roots. Then just stamp each foot a couple of times and say mentally or orally: 'I am now grounded in my everyday life, safe and secure within my own energy, and fully under my own control.' You are now fully grounded and balanced. Go and make yourself a cup of tea or coffee.

My book, *The Medicine Way*, describes how the human energy-system is structured, and how the physical body is surrounded by, and interpenetrated with, a force-field which might be described as the Energy Body and which is comprised of very fine threads of energy. The chakras covered earlier are power centres in this Energy Body. In addition there are control centres in the Energy Body which might be likened to organs of the physical body. The central control centre is located in the navel region, the centre from which you were literally knitted together as a physical being in your mother's womb.

It is from this control centre that threads of light energy can be projected out, much as a spider spins its web and make connections with other webs from other centres. Experience it for yourself.

EXERCISE 13:   Projecting your fibres

Stand at least 10–12m from a clear wall, free from obstruction. If you are inside a large room, move aside any furniture. If you are outdoors, make sure there is a clear patch between you and the wall.

Take in a supply of vital force by practising the Shamanic Breath exercise on page 39 for a few minutes. Then visualize a thin thread of light snaking out from your navel in front of you. Mentally direct it towards the wall and in your mind's eye 'see' the end of it adhere to a place on the wall, level with your chest.

The imagination is the 'eye' of the Hidden Self, and what is 'seen' in the imagination has a reality of its own. The imagination activates the vital energy that you have just taken in, and since there is a Cosmic Law that energy follows thought, the subconcious mind will energize the thought from that energy. The fibre of energy is actually 'there', whether or not it can be seen with the physical eyes. It is only a matter of developing the senses in order to *know* that it is there.

Using the visualized fibre as if it were a thin but remarkably strong rope, pull yourself towards the wall, using the right hand in a series of pulling motions as you walk forward. You may, if you wish, use both hands one after the other, as if climbing a rope. As you move you should feel as if the invisible fibre is actually supporting you and taking the strain of some of your weight.

Continue the exercise out of doors where there is a fairly steep hill. Project fibres from your navel to a point at the top of the slope then, using the invisible cord as a support, pull yourself up the incline. You should find that it takes less effort than it does to walk up the slope normally. This is because the fibres have given you support and therefore the task requires less energy.

If you get no response at first, don't be concerned. Leave it, and try again later. The experience will come if you persist. Make sure, though, that on each occasion you are on your own. You don't want to be inhibited by what others may think.

In this exercise you have been making use of four components that are essential in all shamanic work:

1. A Force or vital power that provides energy.
2. A substance through which that energy can operate. In this case it is the fibres that are composed of aetheric light.
3. The exercise of Mind in order to fashion the thought and shape the intention. In this instance it is the Hidden Self (the subconscious) acting on the instructions of the conscious mind.
4. The individual spirit. An intelligent being to direct both the thought and the intention.

CHAPTER FIVE

'Medicine' Tools

LET US PAUSE FOR A WHILE to consider the 'tools' shamanist's use. These are 'medicine' implements – power objects – that connect the consciousness with the deeper levels of potentiality and creativity that lie within, and with natural and cosmic forces that are without. They are aids to help bring out one's own personal 'medicine' – one's own spiritual power-ability. They are more than just 'implements', for each medicine tool is both an expression of an inner potential, and a means by which it can become manifest.

It should be borne in mind that the power referred to does not lie within the objects themselves. They are but channels through which the vital energy accumulated by the shaman can flow and be more readily directed. The power-energy is within the person using the objects, which are an extension of that person.

The tools I am about to describe are arranged in alphabetical order, but this arrangement is in no way intended to suggest their relative importance in shamanic work. Each plays a vital role.

ALTAR

A shaman's altar is a very simple affair – just a cloth on which tools, implements, and stones and crystals can be laid out ready to hand. It serves as a focusing areas – a portion of sacred space where the visible and the invisible realms merge.

Tribal shamans set up their altar on the ground and sat cross-legged in front of it. Such a posture may be uncomfortable for any length of time for most of us, so the altar cloth may be laid out on a raised surface – a coffee table, perhaps, or any other solid surface one can sit at. A plain linen cloth of a single neutral colour (black or white) is ideal, although some people prefer fabric with decorative fringes and even embroidered patterns. I use a small handwoven rug which rolls out easily and lies flat. It is suitable both on the ground or to cover the surface of a table. What feels right is what is best for you: there are no hard and fast rules. Sacredness of intent is in the mind.

CANDLE

Throughout history candles have been an important symbol tool, and candle-burning a simple and very ancient rite with deep spiritual significance. The candle flame represents not only the Light of the Source of every thing in existence, but also our own individual Inner Light – the centre and source of our own Being. It is also Fire acting in a protective and illuminating mode.

As a preliminary to shamanic work, a candle should be lit as if from one's own Inner Light. This will indicate to the subconscious Hidden Self that there is a switch in conscious activity, from the mundane to the spiritual, when it is lit. Extinguishing the flame at the end of such work indicates a return to everyday reality. The candle is usually white to symbolize purity of intent and to symbolize the powers of Light and Life.

In group work a candle is normally burned at the centre of the circle, sometimes alongside a small vase of cut flowers symbolize the Powers of Love and Law.

DRUM

The drum is a treasured possession for it is the shamanist's access to

Other-worlds. The most commonly used is the round hand-drum which can be carried easily and held by one hand. It is usually made from the wood of a hollowed-out tree trunk or log, and has animal skin stretched over it. In the old days, buffalo skin was preferred by American Indians; today goatskin or deerskin are the most common materials.

The underskin of the drum usually has strips of leather stretched across it, arranged like the spokes of a wheel. The centre, where the 'spokes' cross, is bound with a small piece of soft cloth or leather to form a 'handle' by which the drum may be held. Sometimes wooden dowels are used instead of leather.

The sides of the drum are often decorated with meaningful symbols and even with feathers and hanging pieces. The surface, too, may be painted with an emblem or animal representation. Once you have acquired a drum, don't be in a hurry to decorate the skin because paint won't come off. Wait until you have fuller understanding of your personal medicine power before you attempt to express it in some way on the skin.

The drum stick is a slender length of wood padded at one end with soft material. The handle itself is usually decorated with feathers or leather strips.

Drumming is used to induce altered awareness so that perceptions are extended to deeper levels in which shamanic work can be done. The drum also represents the spiralling power that is associated with the Life Force. The beat of the drum synchronizes the heartbeat – the rhythm of your own Life Force – with the rhythm of the Cosmos, the 'heartbeat' of the Universe. The monotonous beat and the low amplitude of the drum sound relaxes the brain and the neurons – the nerve cells – which then come into tune with the vibratory rates of the invisible worlds.

The human brain is a complex and intricate web of interconnected neurons which serve as connectors with other cells, enabling information to be transported by means of impulses of electrical energy in normal consciousness. In a shamanic state of consciousness a different kind of information is transported. Medical science has estimated that the human brain contain some 10 billion neurons – about as many cells as there are stars in the Milky Way galaxy, and three times the number of human beings on Earth today. Although the frequency range for most shamanic work may be between 160 and 220 beats a minute, the precise rate that will trigger a switch in consciousness will depend upon one's own personal rhythms.

Drums suitable for shamanic work are best purchased from specialist craftsmen who have an affinity with shamanism. A list of possible suppliers is given in the Resources Directory.

FEATHER

A feather is structured like the fibres of the human aura, and can be used by the shaman not only to move air in a chosen direction but also to smooth out auric fibres. This is why a feather is frequently employed as a healing tool. Our auric fibres can become matted and entangled like human hair. Movement of a feather in the skilled hands of a shaman 'combs out' the auric fibres and puts them back in proper alignment. To do this the shaman must be able to see, sense or feel what is wrong.

Feathers were regarded as messengers or energies and greatly prized by American Indians as conveyers of meaning. But here we are concerned solely with their function as a shamanic tool.

FEATHER FAN

You use a feather fan to waft smudge smoke over yourself and others, and also to fan cleansing smoke over medicine objects. American Indians often used the feathers of eagles and other sacred birds, but the feathers of any native bird are suitable. They are attached to a wooden handle that is covered in soft leather or fabric and decorated with beadwork patterns, and with symbols and emblems that are significant to the owner.

MASK

A shamanic mask is a means of allowing inner potentials to find expression, usually in a ceremonial or shamanic dance or other special occasion when it is necessary to ground such energies. A mask may represent an animal, an ally, a guide or Other-world teacher, and is worn in order to make the inner contact more powerful. It may be made from a variety of materials, and be worn on more than one occasion. A simpler type of mask is just painted on the face.

MEDICINE BUNDLE

A medicine bundle is a small pouch worn round the neck or attached to the clothing, and containing items representing the shaman's personal 'medicine'. These items represent also the four kingdoms – mineral, plant, animal and human – and might include images or symbols of personal and clan totems. They may be small stones and crystals, herbs, leaves, bark, small pieces of fur, feathers, teeth, claws, human hair, nail clippings and a specimen of blood.

The medicine bundle is a means of making 'connections', and of bringing the wearer into harmony with other levels of being within the Great Everything.

MEDICINE SHIELD

The medicine shield had nothing to do with protection in battle. It was a personal shield which declared its owner's sacred intentions and connection to shamanic energies – his 'medicine' or spirit power. As such it was treasured by the American Indian.

The personal shield was made of animal skin or hide stretched over a wooden hoop. Around the edges were attached feathers, fringes, and sometimes other dangling objects. It had special emblems and symbols painted on it which indicated the owner's special qualities and quest in life.

It could show a representation of an animal or animals with which the person was particularly related and which represented his principal power source and protection. The colours used also had significance.

You can make your own medicine shield from chamois leather or fabric stretched around a wooden embroidery ring. Your shield is intended to be a mirror of the self, reflecting what you are and expressing in some way the dreams or aspirations you want to bring into being. So it serves also as a reminder of your mission in life – your soul's path – as you presently perceive it. Making your own medicine shield can be a valuable lesson in shamanic understanding because it will help you to recognize your own 'medicine' power and how also to express it.

In Indian tradition a physical lifetime is a 'dream' of the High Self. Making a medicine shield is considered a means of making contact with the High Self for the purpose of 'dancing the dream awake' – bringing into material reality the 'dream' or intention of the soul and thereby fulfilling the soul's purpose.

The medicine shield is not a static thing. It can be added to, developed, and even changed as one's life unfolds and one's 'medicine' alters.

NECKLACE

A shaman does not wear a necklace simply for decoration. The circle of the necklace represents the shaman's own circle of self, and the beads, bones, teeth, stones or other objects strung on it are connections with the owner's own subtle energies.

PENDULUM

For thousands of years shamans of various cultures have used a pendulum as a diagnostic tool. This consists of a small weight – like a crystal or stone or wooden bob – suspended on a thread or thin cord. The thread is held between the forefinger and thumb 7–8 cm (about three inches) above the weight. A circular motion of the bob (either clockwise or anti-clock-wise) and its horizontal or vertical oscillation provides a positive, negative or neutral response to a specific question held in the mind.

A shamanist uses the pendulum as a means of communication between the conscious and the subconscious, and of conversing with the Hidden Self. It is a method of finding out about things which cannot be reached so immediately through the limited faculties of the conscious mind.

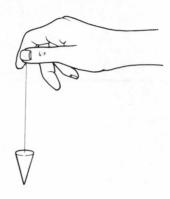

The pendulum can be used for evaluating a condition, locating the region of malfunctioning and disharmony in the human body, determining a beneficial diet, indicating areas of auric or chakra imbalance, and so on. It can be employed as a dowsing instrument to locate sources of water or minerals. Indeed, there is an almost endless list of possibilities.

POUCHES AND POWER BAGS

Shamanists keep a collection of crystals, stones, herbs, and so on, in pouches so they are easily transportable and readily accessible, and sometimes these small pouches are carried in a larger shoulder bag. Although these all come in different shapes and sizes they are usually made from soft leather or hard-wearing fabric. They are decorated with fringes and beadwork, and embroidered or painted with patterns and symbols that have relevance to the owner.

Drawstrings of thick cord, or leather thongs, are usually attached through the neck of the pouch to prevent its contents spilling out.

Pouches and bags are power objects in themselves for they are the repositories of objects of personal power.

PRAYER ARROW

The American Indian considered an arrow as more than just a weapon for hunting game or for fighting tribal enemies. It was a spiritual tool used for stalking food for the soul and defeating tyrants of the spirit. An arrow was often specially made and personalized with emblems and tokens of the owner's power sources, and used as an aid to meditation and as a focus for petitions to the Inner Spirit. A written repetition describing what is required to be manifested in order to enhance one's spiritual life is bound to the shaft.

The shaft of the arrow, cut from the straight branch of a tree, represents the element of Earth and the physical body and is symbolic of manifestation. It is an indication of the strength and fitness of life itself.

Wet rawhide was used for binding the arrowhead and the flight of feathers to the shaft, and this represented the element of Water. As the rawhide dried it shrank tight to hold the head and the flight firmly to the shaft. Such a binding was likened to the tightening of the spiral force and to one's own emotional energy.

The Indian fashioned the arrowhead from stone, or from metal tempered with fire, so the arrowhead represented the element of Fire. It was a reminder that the Fire energy is good when used wisely but that it can be dangerous.

The flight of feathers directs the path of the arrow through the element of Air and represents the spirit, for it is this that controls all aspects of the being from its sacred place within.

As a medicine object, the prayer arrow can be used in outdoor shamanic work to form the centre of a working circle. The arrowhead is buried in the ground, and the arrow becomes the focal point.

RATTLE

The rattle is an ancient sonic device which is used to create an atmosphere of expectancy in a process of change from one level of reality to another. It is primarily a tool of transformation. A rattle is usually made from dried gourds or from rawhide and contains seeds, beans, small pebbles, and sometimes small crystals, and these cause a rattling sound when the instrument is shaken. The gourd is attached to a stick handle which is usually decorated with symbols that are meaningful to its owner.

The shaking of the rattle has great significance. It symbolizes the vibratory movement of the Cosmic forces that expand in all directions and give rise to Law, and so acts as the 'word' of divinity. The rattling sound gently relaxes the mind and slows the brain pattern, so removing the barrier between perception of the material world and the realms of spiritual realities. In other words, it serves as a bridge between the 'worlds', which is why a rattle is of such comfort to a baby.

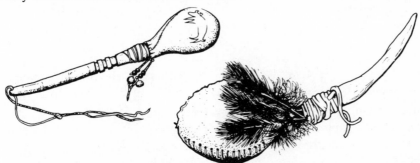

Repeated shaking of the rattle is a signal to the consciousness to switch to an altered frequency level. It can be used as a preliminary to drumming with the drum in order to reinforce the drumbeat, or even as an alternative to the drum. Its sonic drive creates a soothing atmosphere which attracts positive and benevolent energies at all levels.

The rattle can also be used as a diagnostic tool in extraction healing work, and to locate areas of energy imbalance within the human entity.

SMUDGE

To 'smudge' is to purify with smoke from sacred herbs. Herbs which were set apart for spiritual work were sage, cedar, and sweetgrass or lavender. Either loose dried or rubbed herbs can be used. They can be place in a receptacle – a shallow bowl or open seashell, where they can smoulder safely – or tied together as a bundle to form a stick which can be held in the hand and ignited. The smoke from the smouldering herbs is then directed by means of a feather fan towards the person (or persons) or object to be cleansed. Sage smoke drives out negative energies, and cedar can be added to attract positive energies. Sweetgrass (a rare herb found only in North America), lavender or yellow bedstraw adds a blessing. The person being 'smudged' draws the smoke towards him as if scooping it with his hands – first towards the heart area, then over the head and finally down to the feet.

TALKING STICK

A 'talking' stick is a staff that is used to help clarify the thoughts so that they can be expressed clearly. It can be anything from, say, 30cm long (about a foot) to walking-stick size. A staff is primarily a connector linking Sky with Earth – elemental Air and the realm of the thought with elemental Earth and practical reality.

Traditionally the talking stick is passed round in a gathering on the understanding that only the person holding it does the talking. It therefore teaches you to be a good listener, as well as enabling you to speak clearly so that others might understand your thoughts.

The talking stick is also an emblem of a shamanist teacher who conveys knowledge and wisdom to those who seek to know.

SMUDGE POT

A smudge pot is a receptacle for containing smudge mix, or in which a smouldering smudge bundle can rest safely. A shallow earthenware pot about the size of a large ashtray makes a suitable smudge pot; better still, a large open seashell can be used.

WHISTLE

The whistle is a signalling device to call on higher energies and help from the shaman's allies and guides in the spiritual world. Native American whistles were made from the wing bone of a bird, usually an eagle. The whistles of European shamans are generally fashioned from turkey bones.

WAND

Although for many hundreds of years, the wand has been a symbol of high office and an emblem of rulership and authority, shamanically it indicates the axis that connects the solstices — the Sun power of the masculine, conceptual, life-giving 'God' force, and the Earth power of the feminine, creative, nurturing, 'Goddess' force. It is associated with the element of Fire and is used to bring that Fire energy into physical manifestation through transmutation. It can be used for 'healing' in the sense of making 'whole'.

The wand is usually made from a length of 'live' wood cut from a hazel or other nut tree. It is about the same length as the distance between the elbow and the fingertips. The shaman seeks not only the permission of the tree before such a surgical operation is undertaken, but also an indication from the tree as to where the cut should be made. By so doing the shaman ensures that the spirit of the tree is not withdrawn from the branch before the cut is made, so that the removed piece is 'live' wood, retaining within it the spirit of the tree.

This piece is carefully and lovingly prepared by removing much of the bark before the carving work begins. Some shamans' wands have a snake carved around the shaft, indicating the constant flowing and spiralling movement of the transformational energy that turns the spiritual into the material. A carved snake may have a crystal placed in its mouth, to indicate the wand's potential in focusing and directing radiant energy. A crystal can also hold and balance energy that is put into it, and can reflect that energy without distortion. So the wand serves to harmonize and focus energy and direct it in accordance with the will of the shaman, much like a laser beam.

Some wands are decorated with feathers, dangling pieces, and even bells, which cause a gentle and soothing sound when shaken. This emphasizes the wand's qualities as a harmonizing tool and as a restorer of balance. Symbols appropriate to the individual shaman are carved and painted on the shaft and sometimes on the butt.

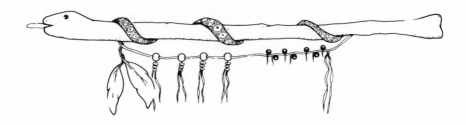

EXERCISE 14: Consecration of tools and objects

Any object that is used as an aid in shamanic work must be consecrated – that is, set aside for the special task for which it is intended – and 'awakened' and charged with power. Shamanic tools are 'brought to life' by having vital energy of the shamanist 'charged' into them, much as a car battery is charged with a surge of power from a mains supply via a transformer. The shamanist is a transformer of energy, lowering its 'voltage' so it can be transferred into objects of wood or stone or crystal and which then become extensions of the shaman and that person's 'medicine' power.

Consecration has three main objectives. First, it cleanses the item physically and purifies it spiritually. Second, it makes it 'special', setting it aside from mundane activity and assigning it to an intended purpose. Third, it dedicates it to this particular purpose. Consecration is more than merely personalizing an object and setting it aside as your own, though it does do just that. And it is more than an extension of yourself on the physical plane. By consecrating, awakening, and charging an object shamanically its existence in non-physical realms is ensured. A shamanic tool can thus accompany its owner on shamanic journeys to other levels of existence, even to other dimensions, for it, too, possesses a non-physical body to make that possible.

The act of consecration is a ritual, and an effective ritual is nothing more than a pattern of actions that can be depended on to get desired results. It must have a clear purpose and be performed with feeling. A ritual without true emotion is of little practical benefit because it lacks essential power. So if you wish to make use of objects for shamanic work and to have tools of your own, you must carry out the consecration with feeling and understanding. Any words you use, whether audible or silent, must come from the heart. The reading aloud of scripted words is just vain repetition and has no power. The outline of a consecration ritual which follows and the words given are intended to prompt thoughts of your own that can be injected with feeling.

Consecration is best performed in an already established power place. If you are acting alone, use your own indoor power spot and set aside half an hour or so when you will not be disturbed.

You will need:

- A white linen or cotton covering cloth.
- A candle, candle-holder and matches.
- Smudge-stick or smudge mix, and bowl.
- A fan, feather or small piece of card to fan smudge smoke.
- A small bowl or container of water.
- A small bowl or container of rock salt.

Place the cloth on a flat working surface – a table top, dressing table or desk top – and stand in front of it, facing North. If this is not possible through lack of space, just imagine that North is in front of you with East on your right and West on your left. The candle in its holder should be placed in the centre of the cloth, with the bowl containing salt or earth on the left (in the assumed West), the smudge bowl behind it (North), and the bowl of water immediately in front of it (South). The item or items to be consecrated should be placed on the right side of the working surface.

As you light the candle, imagine that it is being lit from a flame within you – your Inner Light. The candle flame thus symbolizes the Light of consciousness, the source of your own being, and also the Divine Light and Source of all that exists.

Purify the environment in which you are working and strengthen your own

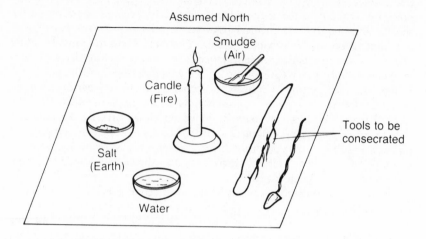

Fig 13. Arrangement for consecration ritual

aura as you learned to do in Exercises 8 and 9. Cleanse the object or articles to be consecrated by fanning smudge smoke over them.

The next step to to accumulate a supply of the vital force within your own energy-system by performing the Shamanic Breath sequence I described at the end of Chapter 4. You are going to transfer this vital force through a shamanic technique and an act of Will into the item or objects to be consecrated.

Purify the water and salt by picking up the bowl of water, and moving it to the space immediately in front of you. With palms down, cup your hands just above the bowl and say emphatically: 'I cast out any impurities and uncleanness in this water to a place where it can do no harm. Go now.' Pause briefly for a moment or two and then say: 'Blessings be upon this water.'

When casting out any impurities or unwanted influences in shamanic work, it is important that they are not left hovering around to possibly affect others. This is a mistake made by some exorcists and occultists in their banishment rites. The shaman ensures that any undesirable influences go to where they can do no harm.

Now move the bowl containing salt alongside the bowl of water. Cup the hands, palms down, over this bowl and say: 'I cast out any impurities or hindrances from this substance of the Earth to a place where they can do no harm. Go now.' Pause, then add: 'Blessings be upon this substance of Earth.' Now take a pinch of the salt and sprinkle it into the water and say: 'Let all good enter into this water that it may bring purity and harmony wherever it flows. So be it.'

'Seal' the action – that is, make it permanent – by tracing a symbol of the Medicine Wheel in the air immediately above the bowl of consecrated water, using your right hand. The Medicine Wheel represents the perfect balance of Force and Form containing within it the symbol of Wakan-Tanka – a North

American Plains Indian name for the Great Spirit that is 'in' Creation and not outside it, and embraces everything that is. Trace the circle by starting at a point immediately behind the bowl and, as you did in Exercise No 9, move your hand in a clockwise motion until it returns to the point where you started. Then trace a line towards you, curve round to the right, then across to the left, and curve clockwise until your hand is back at the starting point again.

Now do the same over the bowl of salt. Return the bowls to their original positions.

It has been stressed by my mentors that as all the elements are involved in shamanic work, shamanic tools and power objects should be consecrated with Air, Fire, Water and Earth to ensure their blessing. So in our consecration ritual all the elements play a part, and before each action we must consider carefully what we are about to do.

Start here

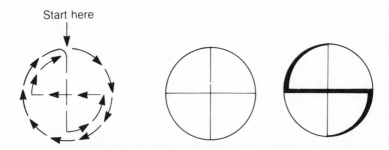

Fig 14. The sign of the Encircled Cross and the Medicine Wheel, and the symbol of Wakan-Tanka

Pick up the first object you wish to consecrate and place it immediately in front of you. Our first action is to consecrate it with the element of Air, and to represent Air we use smoke from smoking herbs. So put the smudge bowl next to the object. Re-light the smudge stick or bowl of smudge mix and fan it vigorously to get it smouldering.

Holding the smouldering smudge in your left hand, pick up the object with your right hand and pass it through the smoke. Do it several times to ensure that the article is saturated in the smoke, and consider throughtfully some of the qualities that Air brings with it. For instance:

Air is freedom and movement. Air is uplifting and exhilarating. Air is lightness and expansion. *Air is mind power.* Say: 'I consecrate you in the Element of Air.'

Next we consecrate the object with Fire by passing it quickly above the candle flame, taking care not to scorch it in any way. Consider what the element of Fire implies: Fire is light and illumination. Fire is radiance and energy. Fire is transmutation. *Fire is spirit power.* Say, 'I consecrate you with the Element of Fire.'

Next comes Water. Dip the fingers of your right hand into the bowl of consecrated water and sprinkle it over the object. As you do so, think about the qualities of the element: Water is fluidity and sustenance. Water is soothing and protecting. Water is diluting and healing. *Water is emotional power.* Say, 'I consecrate you in the Element of Water.'

Now Earth. Take a pinch of salt with your right hand, sprinkle it over the item being consecrated and consider the qualities of Earth: Earth is inertia and solidity. Earth is fertility and abundance. Earth is attainment and achievement. *Earth is physical power.* Say, 'I consecrate you in the Element of Earth.'

Finally we impart into the object qualities of the fifth element from which the four others are derived — the Love 'substance' some call Aether. We also transfer the mana force we absorbed at the beginning of this ritual, by breathing into the object in a deliberate and meaningful way. So pick up the object in both hands, hold it near your lips, and blow hard onto it. This action 'awakens' the object and vitalizes it for shamanic work. *Aether is love power.* Say, 'I consecrate you in Love, and awaken you with the vital breath, that all your works may be performed in Love and fulfilled by Love.'

Now the intention and purpose is spoken into the object: 'I require you to aid me in my cleansing work' (in the case of a feather fan), 'diagnostic work' (in the case of a pendulum), 'magikal* work' (in the case of a wand), and so on. Then take another breath and expel the air from your lungs by saying 'H-ah' over the object. 'H-ah' means 'breath of life', and also the number 4 which is the number of manifestation held in balance and harmony.

Now trace the sign of the encircled cross over the Medicine tool and say: 'So it *is*'.

Lay the article down. The consecration and charging is now complete. If you have more than one item to be consecrated repeat the above ritual. Each tool has been purified by the Elements and enhanced by their power, and each has been energized with vital force for shamanic work in all levels of existence and dimensions.

When you have finished, consider before you snuff out the candle that its flame is being returned to the place of your Inner Light within, and the room restored to normal mundane activity. Keep the consecrated water in a small bottle for future use, or take it outside and pour it into the ground as an offering to Mother Earth. The salt should also be given to the Earth.

---

*Magikal. This is a deliberate spelling to indicate the difference between the magik of bringing into being desired changes, the magic of illusion and trickery and the magick of the ceremonial occultist.

CHAPTER SIX

Totems and Allies

A DICTIONARY DEFINITION of a totem is that it is a natural object used by American Indians as an emblem for a family or clan. Actually, totems are much more significant than that and much more relevant to life. Totems can help us to understand ourselves. They are both connectors to our own inner dynamics and reflectors of the 'substances' of which the personality of our temporal Human Self is composed. In other words, totems can help us to understand why we are as we are and point us to the strengths and weaknesses of our own characters, revealing to us what we lack as well as what we inherently have. Totems can alert us to our own inner potentials so that we can awaken and express them, both for our own pleasure and self-fulfilment and also for the benefit of others.

Some totems are represented in animal form because human qualities and attributes indicated by the totem are demonstrated by the characteristics and habits of that particular animal. Do bear in mind that American Indians – and our own native ancestors – lived very close to Nature and were familiar with the ways of wild animals. But animal representations are not the only form of totems. There are mineral and plant totems too, and these also connect to different aspects of ourselves.

So knowing our totems is a considerable help in coming to understand ourselves. And, of course, if we can come to know the totems of other people we can better understand them, too. So totems can be an aid to better human relations.

My book *Earth Medicine* gives a detailed description and explanation of animal, plant, and mineral totems related to the time of the year of one's birth. These are the totems with which we start out in life. Others are 'collected' along life's journey as we develop. *The Medicine Way* explains further how our individual totems may be used to gain mastery over one's life. Since I have covered the function of totems fairly thoroughly in these two books I shall not take up space here to repeat that information. But I must emphasize one important point. Although animal totems can play an important part in our personal empowerment – the development of our inherent abilities – they should not be confused with 'power' animals. Power animals have an entirely different function and purpose as I shall explain in detail in Chapter 9. So, totems are like 'psychic' sensors which connect us to and reflect aspects of ourselves.

In addition to totems, which were usually well represented on the shaman's tools and implements, the shaman had what were called 'Allies'. Allies are active helpers who co-operate in a mutual endeavour; in other words, they help a shaman in his work. And they can help you, too, in your daily life. So let us examine allies.

An ally might be defined as a 'relative' from another kingdom or realm of existence – be it animal, plant, or mineral – which co-operates with the shamanist in mutual endeavour. Now when rocks, plants and animals are regarded as 'relatives' – as brothers and sisters and cousins who are all 'children' of the same Great Spirit – our attitude toward them can no longer be one of exploitation and dominance. They are seen in a new light, as expressions of the Creative Source, just as we are. As a result, a natural relationship develops between us. We can now be mutually supportive – human and animal, human and tree and plant, human and rocks and stone – as within a family bond, and thus further our individual evolutionary spiritual development.

By engaging help from another plane of existence and seeking to integrate it into or own, as a shaman does, we establish a positive contact and become allied in mutually advantageous endeavours.

A shamanist has three principal allies in the mineral kingdom. These are: rocks, stones, and crystals, and they are aids to both knowledge and healing. In the plant kingdom there are certain trees, plants, and herbs which are aids to attaining equilibrium and harmony. And in the animal kingdom there are allies that function as guardians and add strength and power. Let me deal with each of these kingdoms in turn and give an insight into the allies that can be found there.

MINERAL KINGDOM ALLIES

Stones are man's oldest 'relatives' because they have been around to witness the history of the Earth since long before human and animal life appeared. This is why American Indians attributed 'Grandfather Rock' with knowledge of the past and the 'wisdom of the Ages'.

Most of us have been schooled into thinking logically rather than intuitively. Our perception of the world has been conditioned by scientific materialism and influenced by a monotheistic religion that regarded spirits as either demonic or as superstitious fantasy. So any idea that a stone should be treated as if it has a life of its own seems strange and even ludicrous.

A shamanic world view is different for it is holistic. Everything is regarded as having life and experiencing life for what it is – be it human, animal, plant, or mineral like a rock or stone. Non-human forms are merely differently organized ways of experiencing life. Each has an awareness of what it is, although that awareness is far removed from human consciousness. Everything thus deserves to be treated with respect because all life is holy – that is, everything has a particular use and function. By having 'allies' a shaman is able to integrate their power-energy – their 'medicine' – into his own unconscious potential which can then be used. A stone ally thus helps in the recognition of the self's unrealized power which needs to be brought into conscious awareness to be made accessible.

Shamanists are likely to have a collection of stones, each of which may be used for a different purpose, like a Medicine Wheel working, seeing into the past, finding lost or forgotten things, knowledge and wisdom, and for healing. Some stones may have a quality which the human has recognized, and he will keep that stone by him until he comes into contact with a person in need of that particular quality. The stone ally will then be given in love, knowing its intrinsic value as a helper to one who is in need of what it can offer.

Once you become engaged in shamanic work you may find yourself attracted to a particular stone while out for a country walk, perhaps, or a stone may be given to you or come into your possession in some way. Though you may be attracted to the stone, or find it appealing, you may now know at the time the purpose for which it may be used. That understanding may come later.

EXERCISE 15: Identifying a stone ally

To find out why a particular stone has come to you, hold it in your left hand and lie down in your indoor power spot. Close your eyes and hold the stone to your navel. This is the centre of your energy-system and where you are able to establish contact with anything in existence. Then, mentally ask the stone why it has come to you.

Although a stone's 'awareness' is entirely different from ours, it is possible to communicate telepathically on a spiritual level. Images in the form of shapes or colours may come into your mind, or a mental picture may form. You may even have a visionary experience which may seem like a dream. Such an experience, though, may not happen right away, so you may need to persist with this exercise over a period of time. The secret is not to 'try'. You merely relax and don't 'do' anything. It is like looking at a blank television screen immediately after switching on and waiting for a picture to appear.

Natural crystals, particularly quartz, have a special relevance to shamans. Shamans employ the help of crystal allies to serve as links between the inner world of the spirit and the outer world of material manifestation. They can also serve as 'bridges' between intention and manifestation, and in this way reflect into being something that was only an idea or a potential within the shaman.

Everything around us may be considered a 'reflector' of some kind. Even people we meet, whether we like them or not, are in some way 'mirrors' of our own selves. The reason we don't recognize them as such is that we don't see those faults or qualities within ourselves. Crystals are particularly powerful reflectors for they are light-bearers. They receive, store, and transmit light. The way they can help us most is by enabling us to discover our inner 'light' that connects us with the Light that is the source-centre of All That Is. So crystals are primarily allies for self-transformation.

Let us consider what a crystal is. It is a mineral in a six-sided geometrical form, always with a point at one end, and sometimes at both. Its atoms are arranged in precise patterns and held accurately in place by enormous energies. These atoms attract and 'magnetize' vibrations. Natural quartz crystals are made from silicon and water subjected to intense heat and pressure, and they form in clusters within the crust of the Earth.

A crystal projects quite a powerful force field around itself. For instance, even a small crystal – say, 5cm long (a couple of inches) – may project a force field of about a metre (3 feet). The larger and clearer or more brilliant the crystal, the more powerful or extensive the force field.

A crystal tends to raise the vibrational level of anything in its vicinity. That is why we may feel uplifted or energized in some way when close to crystals. Quartz crystals have high and exact rates of vibration which resonate in harmony with other vibrations with which they come into contact. An energy current can be set up in a crystal and carried to a required destination simply by the intention of the human will. This was part of the secret knowledge of the ancients. In this way a crystal can influence vibration and thereby manifest required change.

Crystals can also be used as aids to meditation, for contacting the Hidden Self and the High Self, for energizing the physical body, for balancing the chakra centres, for developing so-called psychic skills, and for healing.

There are many varieties of quartz crystal. They include clear crystals like rock quartz, or coloured ones like blue quartz, rose quartz, smokey quartz, amethyst – which is purple – and agate, onyx, jasper and opal. Each colour and each stone has its own rate of vibration and its own characteristic powers. So, for instance, amethyst might be used for meditation and illumination, rose quartz to improve and strengthen human relationships, tourmaline to increase personal confidence, agate for emotional uplift, and onyx for practicality.

Since every crystal vibrates at a different frequency depending on its size, shape, and other factors, it is important to ensure that a crystal matches not only your own rate of vibrations but the particular purpose you have in mind in requiring it. This is what some people call 'attunement'. So before choosing a crystal it is important to consider very carefully why you want it and for what purpose. Is it for a place on your Medicine Wheel? Is it primarily for meditation? Is it for inspiration and enlightenment? Is it to aid your search for new knowledge? Think on these things before setting out to choose a crystal.

CHOOSING A CRYSTAL

Should you be presented with a selection of crystals from which to make a choice, just close your eyes and seek inner guidance. Remind yourself of the purpose for which the crystal is intended. Then open your eyes and pick up the first crystal your eyes are drawn to. That will almost certainly be the one you have need of at that moment of decision.

Whilst you had your eyes closed your intuitive faculty will have chosen the right crystal for you before reasoning 'surface' mind had a chance to react to the situation and to go on 'appearances'.

A crystal may come to you in some other way – as a gift, or through some chance encounter, perhaps. In that case, follow the same procedure I described for a stone in Exercise 15 and seek inner guidance as to the use it should be put.

CLEANSING A CRYSTAL

Before using a newly acquired crystal it will need to be cleared of any negative energies and unwanted influences. In its travels from its original location, it is likely to have been handled many times. So it is like a mirror whose surface has been obscured by greasy fingermarks and by dust and grime. Cleansing techniques vary between different schools of thought, but shamanic ways are perfectly natural and there is no exception with crystal cleansing.

Since water is a recognized universal cleanser, washing a crystal under cold, flowing water is a natural way of removing unwanted energies and contamination. Simply hold the stone under a running cold-water tap or in a gently flowing stream or waterfall. First keep its tip upright, then its base uppermost. Throughout the operation be clear in your mind that unwanted energies are being carried away to a place where they can do no harm. This is important because crystals respond to the intentions of their users. After the washing, leave the crystal to dry by placing it near a window for at least a day and a night. If you can plan the cleansing to take place when the Moon is waning, preferably during the phase preceding a New Moon, you will have chosen the most effective period for banishing unwanted influences.

The next stage of the cleansing process is to smudge the crystal with smoke. Simply light your smudge mix or smudge bundle and pass the crystal several times through the wafting smoke. Finally, clear the crystal with your breath. You do this by taking a deep breath, puckering the lips, and exhaling slowly at the base of the crystal as you hold it in your hand.

TUNING A CRYSTAL

Tuning a crystal brings it into harmony with your own vibratory pattern. To do this, hold the crystal in your right hand and with the point upwards. Touch the point with the palm of your left hand, then move the palm away very slowly until it is about 3 to 5cm away (1½ – 2 inches). Then slowly rotate the crystal clockwise until you feel a slight resistance like a screw being tightened. Stop when you feel this for it is an indication that alignment has been achieved and that the crystal and yourself are in attunement.

PROGRAMMING A CRYSTAL

Crystals respond to the intention of the human will, so it is necessary to first programme a crystal to be of benefit only to yourself and chosen others. Programming a crystal is a simple process of instructing it. Hold the crystal close to your mouth and say: 'I instill you with love and for use only for my highest good and for those for whom it may be used.'

Hold the crystal firmly with both hands and gaze into it, concentrating your thoughts on how you intend to use it. Take a few deep breaths then slowly exhale through the mouth and 'blow' your intention into the crystal, empowering it as you do so with your own transformed 'mana' energy.

To check that the intention is now 'locked' within the crystal, hold it up to one ear. If you hear a delicate high note, the crystal has received the message. If not, go through the procedure again.

Crystals used for meditation enhance the experience and can help you to gain a greater depth of inner peace and spiritual understanding. To meditate with a crystal, simply hold it in your hand and focus your intention upon it. The crystal, by its very nature, must respond and it will do so by including an energy that is complementary to meditation. Crystals used in healing reduce stress and tension and have a re-energizing and vibrant effect.

A crystal should always be cleansed after each use, but it does not need to be reprogrammed.

PLANT KINGDOM ALLIES

In American Indian mythology plants were the first child of the union of Grandfather Sun and Grandmother Earth. Trees and plants were regarded as the great 'givers' on the Earth, for they absorb carbon dioxide and negativity and emit life-giving oxygen to enable animals and humans to breathe. They not only provide beauty and harmony but are the source of herbal medicines. Furthermore, plants give of their entirety by offering themselves as food for animals and humans.

Trees and plants are our spiritual relatives, too, and can be integrated into our own lives as allies and special helpers if we will seek their help in a loving way. A tree or plant is an expression of the mind of the Great Spirit *in one place*, and being rooted and immobile, it is also an expression of the place where it grows.

It is fairly easy to obtain knowledge of the physical aspect of trees – their biology, structure, life-cycle, habitat and characteristics – from books, but knowledge of their spiritual aspect can only be found spiritually. So let us now examine this latter side.

In ancient times every tree was a symbol of the connection of the physical and temporal with the spiritual and eternal. Its roots penetrated into the darkness of the Earth – symbolic of matter – and its unfolding branches reached up to the sky and Sun, symbolizing the light of the spirit. Indeed, the Roman occupiers of ancient Britain sometimes referred to Celtic Druids as 'knowers of trees' because they were often observed apparently talking to trees and worshipping their gods among trees. What these ancient peoples recognized was the inner reality of trees so they were not only able to communicate with them but to establish a working partnership.

Shamans recognize that trees have a Spirit, as we do – an intelligence whose experience of existence, though very different from ours, is no less real. Indeed, since trees as a life form have existed on Earth for much longer than mankind, it may be that they are more advanced along their evolutionary path than is man on his! In any event, shamans recognize that trees vibrate in tune with the Earth and associate them with age and wisdom.

A tree spirit, unlike a human spirit, remains in one place. However, if a partnership is formed with a human, it can attain a certain mobility and thus extend the range of its awareness. It does this by giving up a part of itself – a branch perhaps – which retains within it the spirit of the tree. Such a piece is referred to by shamans as 'live-wood'. When a tree is being uprooted or cut down, the tree spirit withdraws its life force. It will even withdraw from a single branch which is being severed, and so that branch becomes 'dead-wood'. The only possible way to obtain live-wood is for the tree spirit to give its permission. If this is sought and granted, the tree spirit will remain in the branch.

The implication of this is important. Trees can be subdivided into parts that have all the inherent and accumulated knowledge of the 'parent'. This means that a piece of live-wood, such as a cutting that will grow into a tree, contains within it the accumulated wisdom of the tree spirit. By fashioning the live-wood into a staff or wand or talking stick the shaman gains access to the tree's wisdom and knowledge, and works in partnership with it.

The partnership is actually between the High Self of the human being and the High Self of the tree, both of which exist in another dimension. On a physical level, live-wood has a different 'feel' from a piece of dead-wood cut from the same tree. This is because the spirit is in it.

At a time in history when Britain and Northern Europe were covered by mighty forests, and trees provided our ancestors with their basic needs of shelter, food and fuel, a shamanic tree lore enabled shamans to tap into a deep reservoir of knowledge and to understand the 'language' of the trees.

In this lore, the qualities of individual species of trees and plants expressed spiritual concepts, and making an ally of the tree and its Spirit was a means of enhancing that quality in oneself. Some of the principal trees and plants and their related qualities are:

APPLE: Sexual love, healing, knowledge.

ASH: Spiritual awareness, intuition.

BEECH: Abundance, affluence, well-being.

BIRCH: Determination, overcoming difficulties.

BRAMBLE: Inspiration, creativity, new ideas.

ELDER: Truth, continuance, timelessness.

HAZEL: Magikal skills, divination, insight.

HOLLY: Rejuvenation, potency, constant growth.

HONEYSUCKLE: Prosperity, attraction.

IVY: Tenacity, persistence.

MAPLE: Enthusiasm, joy, relationships.

MISTLETOE: Fertility, potency, creativity.

OAK: Strength, security, wisdom.

PINE: Spritual growth, emotional strength.

REED: Finding direction, adaptability.

ROWAN: Discernment, protection.

The plant we can most readily relate to at first is our birth totem — that is, the plant that is associated with us at the time of our birth on the Wheel of the Year. My book *Earth Medicine* explains birth totems in considerable detail. A birth totem either shares similar qualities and attributes, or has characteristics which are needed for us to balance and harmonize our personalities. Plant totems related to specific times of the year and their principal qualities are as follows:

21 March – 19 April	Dandelion	Healing
20 April – 20 May	Wild clover	Stability, sustenance
21 May – 20 June	Mullein	Versatility
21 June – 21 July	Rose	Protection
22 July – 22 August	Raspberry	Cleansing
23 August – 21 September	Violet	Practicality
22 September – 22 October	Ivy	Tenacity
23 October – 22 November	Thistle	Strength, endurance
23 November – 21 December	Mistletoe	Renewal
22 December – 19 January	Bramble	Transformation
20 January – 18 February	Fern	Adaptability
19 February – 20 March	Plantain	Harmonizing

Bear in mind that 'medicine' is the spirit power of a particular life form. The best way of discovering the power of a plant is to ask it to reveal its 'medicine' to you! Here's how:

EXERCISE 16:   Finding a plant's 'medicine' power

METHOD 1

Go to a place where the particular plant grows naturally and spend time there. Let the plant know how precious it is to you. Voice your thoughts, or if you can't bring yourself to do this, say the words mentally. Then ask the plant to reveal to you something of its spiritual nature. Wait for an answer. Try to keep an open mind after you have asked your question – like a blank screen. The answer will come to you telepathically as an image or thought in your mind. Write down whatever impression comes to you. Don't attempt to analyse or interpret; that will come later in a meditation session when you get home. Just capture the impression.

Then explain to the plant that you need its help and you want to take a small cutting from it. Allow yourself to be guided where that is to be. Take your cutting and smear a little spittle from your mouth over the wound on the plant. This is both a healing gesture and an offering of yourself to the plant. If it is possible, and you are unlikely to be disturbed for a few minutes, lie down on the ground or grass nearby and relax, holding the cutting to your navel. Close your eyes and ask the plant to reveal its 'medicine' to you.

Again, make a note of any images or impressions that come into your mind or of any dream-like visionary experience. You can extend this exercise by asking the plant what it wants to teach you. You can also develop it further by asking how it can help to transform your weakness into strengths. And you can ask what other plants can become your allies. If it is not possible to perform this exercise by the plant itself, then wait until you get home and choose a convenient time to perform it in your indoor power spot.

METHOD 2

Take a walk into a woodland area with the clear intention of developing your shamanic interests by becoming more attuned to the spirits of Nature and of obtaining a Tree helper. Don't go with any preconceived ideas of what to expect, nor with the intention of linking with a particular species of tree. You are going in a very receptive frame of mind, and with the intention of letting a tree 'choose' you, rather than you choosing a tree. As you walk, try to be aware that there is a non-ordinary, as well as an ordinary, reality all around you, though it is mostly 'hidden' from the physical senses. It means being aware of other living beings, each an intelligent expression of the Great Spirit, each experiencing life differently from you, yet each aware of its own existence.

Walk in whatever direction you feel drawn. Pause frequently to absorb the atmosphere; look around, watch, listen. Continue in this way until you feel drawn to a particular tree. It may be its fragrance that attracts you, or a branch waving in the breeze. The tree is responding to the spirit of your intention and making itself known to you. Go up to the tree and put your arms around it. Give it a hug. Have a loving attitude toward it: admire it; talk to it; tell it you desire only its good and well-being. Then ask for its help. Explain that you want it to reveal its real self to you.

This is going a stage further than sensing a tree's aura and gathering its energy, which you learned to do in Exercise 5. This is an attempt to discover for yourself a tree's inner reality — what it *is* rather than what it *appears* to be. If, with your arms around the tree, you lean your forehead against the trunk, the tree may 'talk' to you. How? Words may come into your mind as the tree's spirit communicates through your 'inner' ears with your spirit. Or the tree may communicate with you visually through an inner 'eye' that is located in your brow. In Sweden, using this method, a Fir tree taught me that trees have a 360° vision, seeing in all directions at once. The field of vision of we humans is only about a third of that.

Try not to reason beforehand about the likelihood of a tree communicating with you. Just have an attitude of expectancy and alertness, and be patient. Then it will happen.

Before leaving, ask the tree to give part of itself to help you in your shamanic work. Again, be patient and wait for intuitive guidance or to be 'shown' in some way. You may have an impulse to pick a leaf from a branch, or to take a cone, a nut, a flower, depending on the type of tree. Or you may feel guided to cut a twig or even a small piece of branch. Should you be led to do this, heal the wound by rubbing some of your spittle over it.

Thank the tree for what it has given, and as a gesture of your love and concern make a token offering before you leave. This can be done by sprinkling a little cornmeal or mixed herbs around the area at the base of the tree from a little bag or pouch which you can take with you. Or you can pull out a few strands of your hair and leave them tied to an appendage of tree bark, or prick your thumb and deposit a spot of blood on the trunk. Even a little spittle will serve the same purpose. It is simply an expression of an exchange of energy.

Don't concern yourself about what others might think about such activities. Keep them to yourself. Other people may believe that plants and trees cannot be communicated with. You will *know* that it is not only possible to talk to trees and plants but that they can in some way 'talk' back!

ANIMAL KINGDOM ALLIES

According to Amerindian mythology the animal kingdom is the second child of the marriage of Sun and Earth. It includes two-legged and four-legged creatures, those that crawl, swim or fly, and also mythological animals. Animals have a clear awareness of their mission and place within the Whole, and act with instinctive clarity, unhampered by either intellect or conscious in the fulfillment of that purpose. Animals, therefore, can teach mankind to become whole-y (holy) again – that is,to regain an awareness of our purpose within the Whole. They can break down our separateness which has not only isolated us from, but made us enemies of, Creation.

Study the behaviour of the physical counterparts of your totem and power animals. Totem animals are those associated with your birthplace on the Wheel of the Year. The ones applicable to you are described in *Earth Medicine*. Power animals are encountered on shamanic journeys and are energy patterns of abilities which enable shamanic work to be performed. These are described fully in Chapter 8. Both totem and power animals are animal allies.

It may not be practical for you to observe their physical counterparts in Nature, but you can find out a lot about them through the books of specialist writers who have made a close study of them. Find out about an animal's ecological function, as well as its behaviour and characteristics, and relate these attributes to the human condition by considering them in human terms. Every animal ally has a speciality and it is helpful in all shamanic work to recognize what that speciality is, so that it can be readily channelled into shamanic endeavour. Power-animal specialities are also covered in Chapter 8.

An animal ally helps a shaman not only to face the difficulties and dangers of physical life, but also to discover a life mission which is a spiritual matter.

A power animal serves also as a guardian, looking after one's interests and security, and as a mediator, too. In shamanic work it is not the shaman's power that is exerted. That would be exhausting and even dangerous under certain circumstances. Power is always exerted from an inexhaustible source and that is where a power animal comes in. It transmit's energy from the power source to where it is required, irrespective of either time or distance. This energy transference is conducted not at a physical but at a spiritual level. It acts first on the etheric or Energy Body via the control centres or the chakra power centres, and then it benefits the physical body.

Two important factors need to be stressed. First, an individual Earth animal – be it a bear, an eagle, a badger, a salmon, or whatever – is only an outward form of the spirit of that entire species. Likewise, a totem or power animal is not an expression of an animal of a power or ability which the animal characterizes.

How does an animal helper communicate with you? Through imagery during a shamanic journey and through internal listening and observance. Remember, the key to shamanic experience is simply letting go and looking and listening.

In what ways can animal helpers assist us? By increasing our physical energy; by providing access to a reservoir of psychic energy; by strengthening our resolve; by increasing our resistance to contagious disease; by sharpening mental alertness; by boosting confidence; and by providing us with a capacity to heal and to harmonize.

CHAPTER SEVEN

The Shamanic Journey

THE SHAMANIC JOURNEY is a technique of experiencing dimensions of Inner Space that lie beyond the five physical senses. It enables the awareness to function at different levels of perception from ordinary physical existence. So a shamanic journey might be more accurately regarded as a change of frequencies, rather than the traversing of spacial distance, in which the consciousness is able to experience non-ordinary realities. It is an experience through which personal empowerment can be obtained, new insight and knowledge gained, and help received in the practical problems of everyday living. Shamanic experience thus has beneficial effects on all aspects of life.

On this visionary journey, the physical body rests (much as it does during sleep) whilst the consciousness (of the spirit) 'travels' into an inner dimension of existence. This is why shamanic journeys are sometimes described as soul journeys since the soul is the vehicle of the spirit.

These journeys are experienced through an altered state of awareness. That which cannot normally be seen and heard because of the limitation of the physical senses, can actually be perceived through 'inner' senses that have been activated. Our physical senses function on a fairly restricted frequency range so our observations and experiences are somewhat limited. It is a bit like having a radio that is equipped only with a medium-wave band; we are unable to receive broadcasts on short- or long-wave frequencies, even though the stations themselves might be quite close to us geographically.

In making such journeys we 'switch' our brain circuits to a different frequency from the one we use in ordinary reality. This produces a change of awareness and a state of shamanic consciousness which is not hypnotic, for the 'traveller' is in complete control of his will and actions at all times; there is no external influence or control. Some describe this condition of shamanic consciousness as a trance, but in my understanding it is not even that, for there is no suspension of sensation or of awareness. Indeed, sensation is actually enhanced and consciousness is expanded. Rather, it is a transcendent state of awareness, which might be likened to a waking dream, except that you are in full control. It is attained through relaxation of the physical body and a slowing down of mental activity and brain wave functioning.

As a result of the pioneering work of German psychiatrist Hans Berger in the 1920s, and Nobel Prize winner Edgar Adrian, a British electro-physiologist, in the 1930s, medical researchers have established that the brain is continuously generating electrical currents which pulse through the brain cells. These can be recorded and measured on a moving graph, and the resulting pattern is called a brain wave. The four commonly seen patterns were given the names of letters of the Greek alphabet. An examination of these four waves can help us to understand that shamanic journeying has nothing to do with the so-called 'supernatural', or a dabbling with the 'occult', but exercises a normal functioning of the brain.

When we are awake and fully alert, the brain is functioning quite fast on what is called *Beta* waves. The Beta state might be described as ordinary consciousness, when normal breathing is around eighteen breaths a minute.

When in a very relaxed state or a light sleep, the brain 'slows' considerably and so does the breathing, to around ten breaths a minute. This is the level of *Alpha* waves. In it consciousness can also experience dreamtime activity.

When the brain slows still further, it enters what is called the *Theta* state. At this level breathing also slows to normally only about four breaths a minute — which is the rate of the shamanic breathing technique you learned in Exercise No 8. The Theta level of brain activity is just above the level of the unconscious. In it there is a heightened degree of visual imagery and mystical experience becomes possible. Theta is a level of shamanic consciousness and access into deeper regions of the subconscious and of the 'connectiveness' with all things. In attaining it shamanically the Theta level is maintained and one stays fully alert whilst it is maintained.

When you are unconscious, in a deep sleep, or anaesthetized, the brain slows even further and functions at which is called the *Delta* wave frequency. At this level breathing slows to only one or perhaps two breaths a minute. It is very difficult to attain a Delta wave rhythm and be awake. Some highly skilled shamans are able to do this, but it requires long periods of training and is beyond the scope of this book. I understand that there are a very few shamans — who in some traditions might be referred to as 'Masters' – so skilled at working at Delta levels that they are even able to transport the molecular structure of their physical bodies to another location. In this way they are able to appear physically to another person or persons in another place. Jesus of Nazareth was able to do this because Jesus was himself a Master shaman!

However, it is the Theta level and the less deep Alpha level that we are concerned with here in attaining access to the Other-worlds of the shaman.

Their landscape has some similarity with the familiar physical realm – there are mountains and valleys, trees and flowers, rivers, streams and lakes, and even oceans – and makes us feel comfortable and secure. But the physical laws or ordinary reality no longer apply. You can defy the law of gravity as you do in a dream. You can fly! Space and distance are no problem for your travel is not merely supersonic, but super-luminary – faster than the speed of light! You can swim like an Olympic champion, dive to great depths without the need of cumbersome underwater equipment, scale high mountains, perform tasks that are beyond the skills of the greatest stuntmen, and even stretch out time – or contract it!

What is observed and experienced in a shamanic journey is just as real and felt just as intensely as ordinary everyday reality. More so, perhaps, because everything that is seen and heard has relevance. Everything that happens has significance – though it may not be fully understood at the time. Even the direction from which things come and go has meaning and purpose in these Other-world experiences.

There is a form of imaginative meditation or guided fantasy which is sometimes confused with shamanic journeying. A difference is that the shamanic journey is undertaken without any preconceived ideas about what is going to be seen and experienced. With guided fantasy or 'pathworking' the essential framework is provided for you, and your imagination is left to fill in some of the details. The experience is thus structured by the originator and it therefore both restrictive and conditioning. For a shamanic journey, however, you are provided only with the means of relaxation that will put you into an Alpha state of being completely at ease yet fully alert. It is true that in both cases the imagination is brought into use. In shamanic journeying the imagination is the impetus that gets you going, the ignition key to start you on your way; but it is not the way itself.

So let us define imagination. Dictionary definitions describe the imagination as an ability to form mental images of external objects. In other words, imagination is an ability to 'image' into life – to allow pictures to form in the mind and to 'come alive'.

Imagination differs from visualization, which is a tecnique that makes wilful use of the imagination to create desired images in the mind. With visualization a deliberate attempt is made to concentrate onforming a clear mental picture of what is required, whereas imagination not only supplies vivid mental pictures but also stimulates the senses – hearing and touch as well as sight, and perhaps even smell and taste. So imagination is not just a matter of image-ing – of see-ing – but of hearing, feeling, smelling and tasting too. With visualization, an image is produced on the screen of the mind in accordance with the will and the desire of the Human Self. With imagination the Human Self steps aside, as it were, and allows images to appear to the consciousness via the Hidden Self.

Imagination requires an attitude of detachment to go with it. It means a 'letting go' of the reasoning faculties of the logical mind which reject what is considered 'not possible' in physical reality based upon past beliefs that have been programmed into it. You need only to watch and listen and respond to what is seen and heard. That is the secret of shamanic journeying – not 'trying', or putting substance on preconceived thoughts. Just watching, listening and responding. This is why relaxation is such a vital preliminary: a gentle turning off from everyday reality and a tuning in to a subconscious awareness. It is like operating a dimmer switch in order to adjust the light gradually. Then the imagination can be activated more effectively and a clearer mental picture created, to establish a link between the physical and the spiritual and act as a launching pad for the journey itself. It is only at the start of the journey that the imagination is treated in this way.

Imagination is more than an activity of the brain or a condition of the mind. It is a very powerful energy which makes anything and everything possible, because it reaches beyond that which is concrete and physical. Whatever has been brought into physical existence in your life existed first in the imagination. Indeed, your life has been limited only by the extent of your imagination! Extend the imagination and more opportunities become available to you, because by exercising the imagination your ability to attain is developed also. What was once beyond possibility comes within range. As a child you made more effective use of your imagination, but later it was programmed out of you by education, through social conditioning as you reached puberty, and subsequently by the attitudes of adulthood. To gain access to Other-worlds you need to recapture and cultivate the aptitude you once had as a child.

As a preliminary to shamanic journeying the imagination is activated by the creation of a clear mental picture of an idyllic place in Nature. There must be either a hole leading down into the ground (in the case of an intended journey to the Lower World) or access to a high point (for an intended journey to the Upper World). It is usually more effective to recall a place that has been encountered during normal, conscious activity and which exists physically. For the purpose of a shamanic journey the location is merely recalled to mind and visualized in as much detail as possible.

A reason for this is that an axis or cord-like 'tube' connects the principal levels or 'worlds'. It is the 'trunk' of the Cosmic Tree of mythology which connects the Middle World of physical existence with an Upper World (its branches) and a Lower World (its roots). Access to this 'trunk' or tunnel exists in the non-ordinary zone of physical Middle World reality, which is why only the initiated could ever find it! The entrance can be almost anywhere on Earth, but access to it can be gained only through an inner reality which lies beyond the physical reality – through the imagination!

Shamanic journeying differs from what is called 'Astral projection', which is a technique of projecting the consciousness out of the physical body and of experiencing the so-called 'Astral' realm. The word 'Astral' is derived from a Latin word for 'star', and was contrived to describe an ethereal-like 'substance', so faint that it was likened to the dimness of starlight, as compared with the soft light of the Moon or the clear light of the Sun. The Astral plane is a dimension of existence closest to the physical. It can be fraught with difficulties, because Astral 'substance' is constantly changing its appearance; furthermore, the Astral is a depository for a great deal of negative energy and malevolent thought forms as well as of spirit entities, who, for whatever reason, are being held close to the physical plane.

In shamanic journeying the 'tunnel' or sky-tube – an inner vortex of energy – conveys the consciousness safely through the Astral much as underground Tube travel in big cities enables the traveller to avoid streets bristling with jostling crowds and busy traffic and reach a desired destination safely and easily.

Before I describe the basic technique of shamanic journeying let us briefly remind ourselves of the cosmology of the shaman, for it is essential to be properly oriented.

Shamans of northern traditions and of some other cultures have an understanding of the Cosmos on four principal levels. The physical reality we are familiar with might be regarded as a 'middle' level. It is the realm of material and environmental space and of physical appearances. 'Beneath the surface' of this middle 'World' is a realm of subconscious activity, sometimes referred to as the 'Lower World'. It is the realm of subconscious dynamics and may also be referred to as 'the Place of Causations'. It is where our own inner dynamics work out their energies into manifestation in the 'World' of physical appearances. It is where empowerment may be obtained. The Lower World overlaps a realm of unconscious activity which is sometimes referred to as the 'Under-world' of 'Place of Potential'. Above the Middle World is a realm of higher consciousness which shamans refer to as the 'Upper World'. It is a 'Place of Inspiration', a realm of creativity and great beauty, and of noble ideals.

In an altered state of consciousness induced by shamanic drumming, spiritual dimensions of existence can be perceived and experienced, and communication with other life forms made possible, because one is being carried along by the Life Force energy that is in all living things. Their

THE FOUR 'WORLDS'

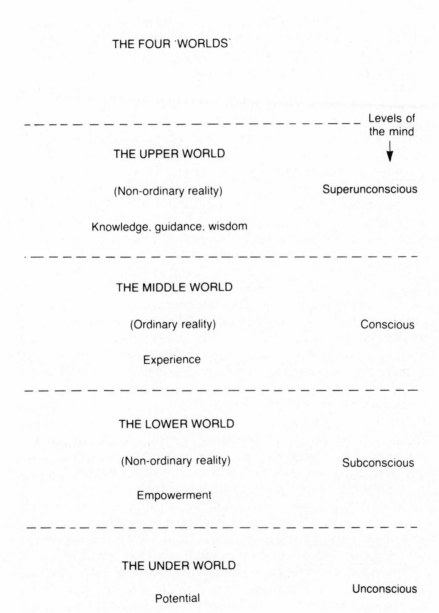

Levels of
the mind

THE UPPER WORLD

(Non-ordinary reality)   Superunconscious

Knowledge. guidance. wisdom

THE MIDDLE WORLD

(Ordinary reality)   Conscious

Experience

THE LOWER WORLD

(Non-ordinary reality)   Subconscious

Empowerment

THE UNDER WORLD

Potential   Unconscious

Fig 15. The four 'worlds'

potencies and qualities are manifested as imagery which has dream-like qualities.

Access to the Lower World is through a tunnel which is, in fact, an opening in a vortex of energy within one's own energy-system. It links the physical realm of 'ordinary' existence to an inner dimension that is oscillating at a speed beyond that of the physical.

Access to the Upper World is by a visionary climb, and transportation through a gossamer-veil or invisible 'tube' 'above the clouds'.

The 'vehicle' on which the journey is made to these Other-worlds is the sound of a shaman's drum. Its regular and monontonous beat conveys the consciousness safely and surely from the reality of mundane physical existence to that of the spirit, and back again.

The drum itself is much more than a sound box. It is symbolic of all the 'worlds', for its frame is made from the trunk of a tree — a reminder of the Cosmic Tree. The drum is circular, to indicate the totality of existence within which all the 'worlds' can be experienced, each being only an aspect of the whole. Its beat is the sound of that totality, that can call everything into being from the Nothing-ness that is the potentiality of existence.

Some drums have thongs of leather stretched across the underneath to provide a hold for the drummer. These are often arranged to form a web of eight strips — the cardinal and non-cardinal directions, the eight spokes of the Medicine Wheel, and eight 'legs' of the mythical horse Sleipner which carried the Norse shaman-'god' Odin to the Other-world, the eight legs of the spider on a web, and so on — with a hold where they cross in the centre.

So it is the drumbeat that carries the shamanic traveller sonically. Its monotonous, regular rhythm is like a heartbeat, and might be described as 'the heartbeat of the Universe'. The rhythm conveys a sense of urgent movement which carries the consciousness along with it, provided it is relaxed into. The consistently regular rhythm and tone of shamanic drumming is carried through the ear to the brain. This adjusts itself to operate at the same oscillation and thereby switches into deeper aspects of the mind to provide access to subconscious and even superconscious levels whilst you are still conscious and fully alert. It allows inner dimensions of spiritual reality to be perceived and experienced, and is a state of being that has been consciously entered by shamans and mystics throughout time.

It is possible to experience shamanic consciousness by using a specially-recorded audio drumming tape on a personal cassette player that is equipped with headphones. This method has practical advantages because it does not require the presence of a live drummer who is skilled in shamanic drumming, nor will it disturb neighbours or others in close vicinity.

I have produced a studio-recorded drumming tape which uniquely combines the heartbeat with multiple drumming, and rattling, and spans a frequency range which appears to be effective for most people. It has been tested under workshop conditions with remarkable success among first-timers as well as experienced 'journeyers'. This tape bears the title *Shamanic Experience (The Tape)* and is obtainable direct from myself, from the publishers of this book, or from leading New Age suppliers and book stores (see Resources Directory). It also has the advantage of incorporating a vital relaxation preliminary before the drumming starts. Deeper, subconscious levels of awareness can then be reached through the drumming.

The change from physical to spiritual reality is thus achieved effortlessly. You don't need to undergo long and arduous training; you don't even have to 'try'. All you have to do is relax into the drumming – just let go and let it happen. Some people experience a gentle up or down movement like being in an elevator, or a slight rocking sensation like travelling by rail. This is because there is an energy-flow both into and out of the physical dimension. Some experience the gentle twists and turns in the tunnel journey, because the vortex channel itself is a spiral.

'Letting go' does not put you into an hypnotic state or under someone's control or influence. You are fully awake and in control at all times. You decide your own actions and reactions, and you can end the experience whenever you choose. All that is required is that you stay alert and watch and listen, much as you do when enjoying television or a movie. On a shamanic journey, however, the eyes are covered to keep out the light and to avoid distractions, so what is seen is with the inner 'eyes' and what is heard is with the inner 'ears'.

Such a journey is a serious undertaking an should never be entered into lightheartedly. A shaman always has a clear intention for embarking upon a journey. It is advisable to limit the first time to just experiencing the tunnel and observing the landscape at the other end. Once you have succeeded in attaining that, you can extend the mission to looking for something of interest to 'bring back' with you.

'Bringing back' something you see on a shamanic journey is an attempt to establish in physical reality what has existed in non-ordinary reality. It means capturing the vision by drawing it, making a representation of it in some way or acquiring an article that looks like it. It is a means of 'grounding' the vision and coming to an understanding of its meaning and significance and relevance to your life. Let me give an example:

Several years ago, on my very first such journey, I was fascinated by what appeared to be a pendant or talisman of some kind, which had a small jewel in its centre. When I related the incident to my mentor afterwards I was asked to draw it, and to make a replica of it. Only then would its meaning become clear. The article seemed to be made of a hard material, apparently layered in some way. It was partly this aspect that had singled it out from the other objects that were with it.

Some days later I was in a London shop that stocks a large variety of semi-precious stones. I was looking for a gemstone similar to the one I had seen on that visionary journey, and came across a display of paintings on oyster shells. When I looked more closely at these small pictures I realized that oyster shells themselves are structured in thin layers. Then it dawned on me. The talisman I had seen was an oyster shell! I acquired a blank shell, and painted on it the design I had seen. I glued a lace agate gemstone, similar to the one I had seen, to its centre. At that time I had no knowledge of the ancient form of angular symbolic writing known as Runes, but I was later to discover that the design was, in fact, a Bindrune – a combination of a number of Runes – which, in this case, integrated nine Runes in its single design and which itself was contained within an eight-spoked wheel. The whole design on a 'layered' structure was thus rich in symbolic meaning.

I consulted as many books on Runes as I could lay my hands on to find the possible meaning of the design, and from this study came up with a 'message' in the talisman which ran to several pages. It also encouraged me to enquire more deeply into the meaning of the eight-spoked wheel on which the Bindrune was impressed, and this led me to a study of the Medicine Wheel and a meeting with an American Indian shaman who taught me some of its basic concepts as a shamanic tool. Later I was to have the privilege of personal instruction on the meaning of the Runes by a Rune-mistress of the northern tradition, which took my understanding further than what had been gleaned from books. Two years later during a visit to Scandinavia I was to meet a Swedish shaman who introduced me to shamanic ways of understanding the Runes. All this from an incident on a single shamanic journey!

On other occasions I have 'brought back' from a journey a feather, pine cone, cactus, flower, twig, stone and other natural objects. In every case obtaining a similar object in physical reality has resulted not only in an understanding of its relevance to me personally, but also subsequent events in my life have brought that meaning into practical realization.

Journeys with more specific purposes, like gaining the courage to face a particular situation, the energy to perform a special task, the wisdom to cope with a difficult problem, the determination to achieve a desired goal, the discovery of a hidden potential or talent, the healing of a personal relationship or even physical illness, are best left until you become more familiar with both the experience and the territory. Before setting out on a 'journey' it is essential to consider most carefully just what you wish to attain from the experience. Generally, if the intention is for empowerment – say, the ability to perform a particular task, develop a trait or quality, deal with a weakness, and so on – the journey should be to the Lower World where empowerment is to be obtained from subconscious and unconscious levels. If you want to receive knowledge or guidance regarding a particular problem or develop creativity, then the journey should be made to the Upper World to meet a Teacher or Guide with whom the issue is discussed at superconscious levels.

Clarify your intention by writing it down. It should be on a single issue and not a conglomeration of matters; in shamanic work you must focus on one thing at a time. Put your thoughts into words, then simplify it until what you have written can be expressed in a single sentence. Like this:

'I am going on a shamanic journey to the Lower World in order to obtain the power to be more confident (or forthright, persistent, patient, caring, contented – or whatever is is you want to be).' Or perhaps:

'I am going on a shamanic journey to the Upper World to seek my Teacher's advice or guidance on … (state the problem).' Or simply:

'I am going on a shamanic journey to the Upper World to seek knowledge about …'.

Your intention should be stated mentally or out loud while you are relaxing before the drumming starts.

Let us now examine in detail a technique for entering an altered state of awareness and experiencing a shamanic journey. If you are working on your own, your indoor power spot, where you can be undisturbed for an hour, is the most suitable location. Place a blanket or something similar on the floor which you can lie on. In addition to your personal cassette player, headset, and drumming tape, you will need the following items of equipment:

- Headscarf or handkerchief to cover your eyes.
- Smudge mix or smudge bundle.
- Smudge pot.
- Rattle.
- Fan.
- Candle.
- Matches.
- Notebook and pen.

Place the candle in a holder in a safeplace where it cannot be knocked over. Light the candle as if from your own Inner Light – the Flame within you. Your Mind Space is now 'switched on' for shamanic work.

Light the smudge mix or bundle and smudge yourself to cleanse your aura. Then smudge the area around you, wafting smoke from the smouldering herbs in all directions as you turn clockwise. You will thus have purified the atmosphere and dispersed any negativities.

Then establish your Mind Space sonically. Using a rattle is a means of tuning the atmosphere to a higher vibrational level in which spiritual work can be performed more effectively. By rattling to the Eight Directions you signal in higher energies and balance them within yourself. By tracing a circle around you, rattling as you turn, you establish a sonic globe which shields out disruptive and negative vibrations.

The Eight Directions are:

- Ahead (say, North).
- Behind (South).
- Right (East).
- Left (West).
- Above.
- Beneath.
- Centre.
- Within.

In recognition of this, the shaman brings all things to his Circle of Awareness in perfect balance and harmony and centres them within himself with Love – the great bonding Force that holds everything in existence together. When this piece of knowledge was revealed to me it was described as one of the great 'treasures' of the Universe.

Here is a basic rattling technique which can be used as a preliminary to any shamanic work to aid the task that lies ahead.

EXERCISE 17: Rattling technique

The rattling technique needs to be practised several times so it can be performed naturally with feeling and understanding. Hold the rattle in the right hand at the base of the handle so that the wrist can be moved freely. The right hand is the active-expressive hand. It is sequentially preferable to begin the rattling by facing East – the direction of the rising Sun and the coming of light. Stand comfortably, feet slightly apart, and with your weight evenly distributed. Squint the eyes to reduce distraction from any brightness of light, and as you move around take small, rocking steps, moving your weight from one foot to another.

Bearing in mind that the Sun is symbolic of the Source of all Life and Light, shake the rattle rapidly for about four seconds. Pause a second, then rattle again for about four seconds. Do this four times. As you rattle, say aloud or silently:

Spirit of the East, where Light come from
Bringer of Life and Light to all living things
Gateway to the Spirit and the Element of Fire
Come into my circle and enlighten me.

Turn to face the South, rattling as you do so. Then give four more shakings of the rattle, saying:

Spirit of the South, where the Sun is strongest
Gateway of the Emotions and the Element of Water
Come into my Circle and strengthen me.

Turn to face the West, rattling as you move, and give four shakings of the rattle, saying as you do so:

Spirit of the West, where the Sun sets
Gateway of the Physical and of the Element of Earth
Come into my Circle and transform me.

Continue to rattle as you turn to face the North. Rattle in that direction four times and say:

Spirit of the North, where the Sun rests
Gateway to the Mind, and of the Elements of Air
Come into my Circle and teach me.

Continue rattling as you turn to face East. Look upwards, rattle four times just above your head and say:

Sky Father above, power of Life and Light
Come into my Circle and motivate me.

Hold the rattle at waist level and rattle four times towards the ground and say:

Earth Mother beneath, power of Love and Law
Come into my Circle and nurture and protect me.

Now seal and centre your working area by turning clockwise and tracing a circle around you, rattling constantly. Complete three circuits in this way – the one at chest-level indicates the Middle World, one at eye-level the Upper World, and a third at thigh-level the Lower World. Then, trace a circle in the air with the rattle, with your arm outstretched. Still shaking the rattle, move it up over your head, then as best you can behind you, down towards your feet, and up in front of you. Next extend your arms to the right and rattle a circle from your right side, up over your head, down your left side towards your feet, and up again to the right. Finally, rattle four times at the level of your solar plexus, and in your imagination draw all these energies within you.

You have now set up a sonic sphere, and embraced all the directions. By calling in their powers you have centred each of them and also brought them within yourself. All eight directions are therefore involved.

Put aside the rattle and lie down on the floor covering in the middle of the space you have just prepared. Use a cushion or pillow to support your head if necessary. If you are using a drumming tape, place your cassette player by your side with the start button in a convenient position. Put on the headset, cover your eyes, and relax. Consider the intention of your mission, and repeat the precise purpose of your journey to yourself four times. Relax, and think about your personal entrance to the Lower World. Get the picture of the tunnel entrance clear in your mind. Then, when you are ready, simply turn on the tape.

When the drumming starts, simply allow yourself to relax into the drumbeat. Imagine yourself at the entrance to your chosen Earth opening and actually stepping into it. Then let the drumbeat carry you along. The tunnel may be just blackness at first, and you may sense a gentle feeling of being pulled along as if on a cushion of air. You may feel that the tunnel twists and turns, or that you are being carried along in a spiral movement. This sensation is warm and pleasant and quite normal. Gradually your 'eyes' may become accustomed to the darkness and you may discern the tunnel walls.

These walls may appear to be ribbed or corrugated and stone-like. If you see markings, drawing, or symbols, try to retain a clear picture of them. Draw them for yourself afterwards. Should you come up against any kind of obstacle or blockage, look or feel for a way round it, and one will appear. Eventually you may see a pinpoint of light in the distance. Make for it. As it gets bigger and bigger and you near the end of the tunnel everything will appear brighter.

When you reach the end of the tunnel, look through the opening and observe the landscape beyond. Then step through the opening. Take a few steps forward and look back to the tunnel entrance. Observe carefully its surroundings. Then have a good look round. Try and absqrb the detail of what you see: the terrain; the flora; the colours. Look around for something of interest to bring back with you — a stone, a jewel, a trinket, or some other small object.

Your signal to return is when the constant drumming stops and is followed by a sequence of four separate drum beats. When this happens, say your farewells and turn back immediately to the opening and enter the tunnel with the object you have chosen clutched gently to the solar plexus. After the return signal the drumming will resume at a much faster pace than for the inward journey. Again, just relax into the drumming and let the sound transport you along. On the return journey you may be surprised at how quickly you arrive back at your starting place outside the tunnel entrance.

When the drumming stops, stretch your limbs and take a few deep breaths before uncovering your eyes. Shamanic drumming has beneficial effects on the human energy-system and on the mind. It stimulates the flow of blood, relieves tension, and encourages regeneration of the body tissues, but it is just as important to relax out of shamanic consciousness as it is to relax into it. So don't be in a hurry to get up. Re-attune yourself to your surroundings slowly. Have a good stretch, then stand up and stretch your arms and legs once more. Write up an account of your experience whilst it is still fresh in your mind. This is not only important for future reference but is also a part of the 'earthing' process.

During the drumming you may become aware of a sound between the drumbeats which compels your focusing to the exclusion of the drumbeat itself. It may be an echo of your own sound or song. Every shaman has a power song, which is an expression of his own energy-system and of potential that lies within.

Everything in existence has its own sound or 'song' — its individual contribution to universal harmony. The sound of some creatures is easily recognized. Different species of birds, for instance, have their own distinctive song. Various kinds of wild animal have their particular call or cry. Similarly, the Soul of every individual human has a vibrational frequency — a sound or combination of notes — which can be resonated as a power song. This is a song of your own, your own combination of notes, with or without words.

My very first power song was just three notes which later, by repetition, extended to six. Words were then added which expressed the intention of the song-sound — to travel shamanically:

I have wings like a bird.
I can fly up on High.
I can reach to the Sky.

How do you find your own power song? One way is simply to listen for a note or notes between the drumbeats or the shakes of a rattle. It takes careful concentration and a little practice. Open your mouth slightly and let a sound come forth naturally. Don't force yourself to produce a sound — be patient. It will probably be a single note at first; then it may change up or down the musical scale, and change again. It is best to allow the notes to express themselves as vowel sounds: *Ahhhhhh; Eeeeeee; Iyeeeee; Ohhhhhh; Oooooow.* Don't concern yourself at first with trying to find words to match the sounds — these will come later. They may not rhyme, or even be poetic, but they will have a special meaning for you.

EXERCISE 18: The power song quest

An effective way to discover your own power song is to go on a Power Song Quest. This entails spending time in an unspoiled natural location where you can be undisturbed and where you can sing out without worrying that others might hear you. Don't limit the amount of time to be spent there. It may need only half an hour, but it may take an hour or two, or even longer. Have a light breakfast or snack before you set out, or, better still, fast. When you arrive at the location, find a spot where there is room to move around without danger of tripping or stumbling.

Sit with your back to a tree and meditate for a while. Concentrate your thoughts on the mission itself. You have come to this place with the intention of finding your own power song. You plan to draw upon the spirit of Nature to help you. Be confident that since you have set your mind clearly on the quest your mission is bound to be a success.

Then spend time just walking around in a circle. Get the feel of the location.

It is a place you have chosen, but paradoxically it is a place that has chosen you and called you to it as if, somehow, 'it' knew what was in your heart. So absorb the atmosphere. Breathe it in deeply. Feel it becoming part of you and you being absorbed in it.

Then concentrate your attention on listening for a sound, and a melody that will come to you from both within and without. It may arise from the song of a bird, the call of an animal, the rustle of leaves in the breeze, or the gentle flow of water in a stream. Let the sound just come forth from within you. Don't be concerned about what it may sound like to others. No one can hear. So just let the sound come out.

What you are seeking is your own 'silent' sound: the melody of your Soul. When it comes, sing it out loud and keep on repeating it. Then let your feet move to its rhythm and 'dance' your melody. You will find a child-like pleasure in so doing. Let yourself go — enjoy yourself.

While moving around, allow words to fit the notes. Just simple words that express a direct statement and can be repeated frequently as necessary.

The melody has thus become a dance, and the dance has become a song — a song of your own source of power. Once found and expressed it can become a powerful and effective aid in shifting your level of consciousness into an altered state in which shamanic work can be performed. You can carry your power song with you on shamanic journeys just by mentally singing it as the drum carries you on your way.

Another effective technique is the shamanic dance. Shamanic dancing stimulates a free flow of bio-energy so that constrictions and tensions are released and power from other levels of existence can be drawn upon and directed into healing and harmonizing, and other shamanic work. Shamans use this dancing to bring into Middle World manifestation something of the energy of their power animals, helpers and guides, and as a means of channelling their visions and dreams — part of the process of 'dancing their dreams awake' so they become physical realities.

The dance has two prime purposes: cleansing and inducing. The cleansing process is achieved on both physical and non-physical levels by releasing not only muscular tensions and energy blockages within the body, but also by freeing emotional, mental and spiritual 'knots' and kinks and getting rid of constrictions and inhibitions. The result of this process is that you always feel good after performing a shamanic dance. The inducing process frees the Spirit from its confinement in material existence so that it can readily transcend to other levels. In other words, shamanic dancing can be another form of shamanic journeying; the consciousness can be altered by it and as a result non-ordinary realities can be experienced during its activity.

To an outside observer, a shamanic dance may not appear to be a dance at all for it follows no pattern. It is a spontaneous movement in any direction. Perform the following exercise and you will experience it for yourself. If you are alone you will need a rattle to provide the sonic drive for the dance. If you are working with a group of people drumming and rattling should be provided, but it is still helpful to do your own rattling.

EXERCISE 19: Shamanic dancing

Before you begin, make sure you have a clear area to work in. Hold the rattle in your right hand and just shake it. Once you have a rhythm going, start to shake your body. Shake the right leg, then the left. Move the hips, then the shoulders. Move the head from side to side. Move the body forward, slowly at first, and then more quickly as you continue to shake the rattle. The idea is not to work yourself into a frenzy, but to allow energy to flow freely through you and to move gently with it. Your steps should be on the flat of the foot rather than on your toes so you maintain a firm and solid contact with the floor or ground.

If you have discovered your power song, let it come forth. You may feel inclined to chant in some way, or even to make animal-like sounds. Simply let yourself go and let it all happen! Continue until you have had enough, then 'earth' yourself by flopping on the floor and relaxing to allow excess energy to be absorbed into the cosmic reservoir.

'Earthing' or 'grounding' ensures a full re-orientation from Alpha and Theta brainwave activity and non-ordinary reality to the Beta rhythm of ordinary reality. Unfortunately many people who engage in mystical, spiritual or psychic activity become impractical theorists and idealists with their 'heads in the clouds', primarily because they lack the balance of practicality. Although shamanism is essentially a spiritual activity it is none the less practical and down-to-earth. Shamans do recognize the need to maintain balance by being fully 'earthed' in the Middle World of physical reality, which is why 'earthing' is so essential after every shamanic activity.

This chapter has concentrated on Lower World journeys since experience of these is preferable before setting out on Upper World journeys. Journeys to the Upper World are similarly from an imagined idyllic place in Nature, but one where there is a high point from which to launch off – a mountain peak or hill-top perhaps, or the top of a tall tree. The first journeys should be limited to just meeting a Teacher or Guide. Only when contact is clearly established should specific questions be put and discussed.

CHAPTER EIGHT

Power Animals

EVERY CREATURE that runs, crawls, swims or flies, has purpose and is an expression of the Creative Source. On shamanic journeys 'power animals' may be encountered which also have expression and purpose. Although a power animal has the appearance of a physical or mythical animal, it has no existence in the physical world. It exists in non-ordinary reality though its effects can be experienced in everyday life. So, although a power animal may be considered 'imaginary' it is 'real' all the same, and is a source of beneficial power.

Let us come to an understanding of what a power animal is and examine its function in the shamanic experience.

Essentially, there are four kinds of power:

- There is power that is an *energizing force*
- There is power that is *might* and has control over whatever it is applied to.
- There is power that is the ability or capacity to do *work*.
- There is power that is the endowment of *authority*.

Dictionaries define an animal as a creature that has intelligence, sensation and movement. So a power animal might be described as a source of energizing power in animal form, with intelligent motion.

A power animal, then, is an expression in animal form of an intangible spiritual energy-force. It is an energy-pattern at subconscious and unconscious levels that has been given life by the human spirit. In other words, the animal form characterizes the nature, attributes and behaviour of an essentially spiritual force, which has the ability to perform certain work and give it expression in material existence.

A power animal is thus an energy-pattern that provides the abilities it characterizes.

These qualities and characteristics are not those of an individual animal, or even the perfected group soul of an entire animal species whose 'echo' is contained within one's own energy-system but an aspect of one's own human nature. It is the Life Force in archetypal animal form which can find expression in human terms. So although a power animal possesses all the qualities of its earth animal counterpart it is supplying physical, emotional, mental and spiritual energy that can be expressed humanly. By connecting to this power source one can draw upon its characteristic qualities.

We all have power animals whether we are aware of them or not. Indeed, we can even 'lose' one through illness, emotional trauma, mental strain or an abuse of some kind. A power animal can be taken away from us unknowingly by another person sapping our energy. Retrieval of a power animal that has become 'lost' is a basic shamanic practice and a form of healing that can restore balance to an individual.

A power animal increases physical and emotional energy and mental and spiritual alertness because the connection that is made is with the power-giving frequency of that particular source. Our auric cocoon and force-field thus becomes more vibrant and functions more harmoniously.

A power animal also helps to resist any kind of harmful intrusion from mental, emotional, or spiritual influences or from physical infections or diseases. Let it be clear: a power animal is not an outside entity. It is a pattern of energy that is within you. It is not something that possesses you. Rather you possess it!

The word 'spirit' has been much confused and abused through religious connotations and terminology, and through superstition and prejudice. Quite simply, spirit is individuated Life Force. The spirit is the source of every physical form's power and expression. There is a spirit within every human, in all animals, all trees, all plants, and within rocks and stones because there is life force in everything, but it is *differently organized*. There is spirit even in the Earth, and in the Sun and the Moon and the stars. So when a shaman talks of 'spirits', he or she is referring to an unmanifest life source that infuses and empowers whatever is manifested.

A power animal is a means of communicating with aspects of your own mortal nature as compared with the 'spiritual' nature of your immortal High Self. A power animal represents a potential, or a talent, an ability or strength, that constitutes an expression of your totality. The purpose of each individual power animal is to bring an understanding of its attributes, and an understanding of what needs to be developed, tamed or trained. Recognition of a power animal does not mean that its attributes are being *used* – only that they are *there* and seeking expression and development. When you identify with a power animal its desired qualities flow more positively within your energy-system. Power animals are providers and protectors of power. They give their power or 'medicine' to supplement and enhance your own, or protect your energy from being depleted through intrusion.

A power animal's primary power source equates with the essential qualities of the physical animal appearance it bears. For instance, a lion's main attribute might be 'strength'; an eagle's 'far-sightedness'; a fox's 'stealth'; a beaver's 'constructiveness'; a turtle or tortoise 'persistence'; a snake's 'transformation', and so on. However, while such generalizations may be helpful, the power animal will usually indicate its main attribute in some way.

In myths, legends and folk tales, animals and sometimes trees and plants are humanized and distinguished by personality characteristics. All life forms converse together as a community within Nature. That is exactly how it is in the non-ordinary reality of the shaman.

Such stories have been handed down from the shamanic roots of our cultural past. They contain a rich heritage of truth regarding the holistic nature of the Creation but which has been obscured from solely material vision.

On a shamanic journey a visionary creature becomes identified as a power animal when it appears consistently. Another identifying sign is that a power animal is always friendly and does not appear to be threatening in any way. It should be asked: 'Are you my power animal?' and allowed to respond in some way.

When a shaman is confronted by a power animal during a shamanic journey he will greet it as a friend and communicate with it as easily as with a human being. So how may power animals communicate with you?

- They may *talk* to you verbally.
- They may convey words to you *telepathically*.
- They may convey *images* to your mind.
- They may lead you to *symbols* which you will need to decode.

What are the specific ways in which power animals may be of help to you?

- By giving you energy, vigour, strength and enthusiasm to meet a challenging situation that is facing you – like job interview, an important meeting that is vital to your long-term interests, a big decision, a sporting event, and so on.
- By supplying you with ideas for a particular project you are working on, or a way out of a difficult situation which is causing you concern.
- By fighting off any intrusions in your body and increasing your resistance to physical illness, especially when there is an epidemic about.
- By speeding your recovery from an illness you may already have.
- By helping you to discover a piece of vital information you may be seeking, or to find a lost object.

- By protecting you from physical harm or injury.
- By improving your relationships with other people.
- By boosting your self-confidence because the energy-force within you is being increased.

Since a power animal has certain characteristics and can provide the ability to perform those attributes, it is essential for practical application to understand from shamanic journeys what these are. A tribal shaman living close to Nature and familiar with the habits of wild animals can quickly recognize the significance of a power animal. Those of us brought up in urban communities and whose knowledge of wild animals comes second-hand — from books, films, videos, and other people — are not able to interpret their messages so easily.

The information contained in the following pages of this chapter is intended to help to overcome some of this difficulty. It should enable you to relate more easily to a power animal, and to recognize its significance in your own life more readily. The animals listed in alphabetical order are those that appear most frequently on the shamanic journeys of non-native peoples. The comments on each are intended not as interpretations but rather as *indications* of their likely meaning. In any shamanic work only you, or your inner teachers, can interpret meaning. All that a shaman or a more experienced shamanic worker can do is to make suggestions or give guidance. Clarification of the intended meaning often comes through real-life experiences, through apparent 'coincidences', through sudden flashes of illumination, or through making shamanic journeys to the Upper World to seek direct interpretation from the Inner Teacher — your High Self.

The imagery perceived on a shamanic journey is a pattern of information which the consciousness is able to carry from one level of being to another where it can be made available for use. This imagery is the language of the Hidden Self and of the High Self aspects of your total being, and has to be translated into the verbal language of the Human Self.

ANTELOPE

Antelope is a hunted animal, so its future is always uncertain. Its major concern is with the 'Now', and with mortality and survival.

As a power animal Antelope stresses the importance of making the best of what you have and of the time at your disposal, and the need for sustenance and nourishment, not so much in a physical sense but mentally, emotionally and spiritually. Antelope can give you the power to strengthen your mind and heart, and to acquire the courage necessary to help you take the right decisions. It emphasizes how important it is to know exactly what you want, and to then make up your mind to do something positive in order to bring it about.

Antelope points to a higher purpose, beyond the obvious. So listen to what Antelope has to tell you on a shamanic journey, and look carefully at what it is trying to show you.

Key indicator: Ability to take decisive action.

BADGER

Badger is a quick and aggressive animal which will fight ferociously for what it wants. It lives in burrows and feeds off the roots of plants. As a power animal, Badger teaches the need to fight for your rights and to defend your principles against any attack.

Badger emphasizes that you should take the initiative in any difficult situation, and not just accept it meekly. If the problem is an emotional one, Badger encourages you not to keep your feelings bottled up inside but to let off steam. Have a good cry. Blow your top. You'll feel better afterward.

Badger is helpful in healing and harmonizing, encouraging you to look for unconventional means if necessary to affect a cure or result. Roots and herbs can help to restore your health. If the problem lies in a work situation, or is one concerning human relationships, the solution can be found at the roots.

Key indicator: Ability to take the initiative.

BAT

The bat is an animal steeped in mystery, and one which arouses unease in some humans because it is related to darkness and the unknown. Some are afraid of it, perhaps because of its association in horror moves with the supernatural and with ritualistic death.

The bat lives in a cave or a dark place; this is symbolic of the womb, and the animal's position hanging upside down parallels that of the unborn self, immersed in darkness. To encounter Bat as a power animal, therefore, signifies the process of initiation – the ending of an old way of life and a rebirthing into a new life pattern. Bat is there to help you to let go of old habits and a previous way of life, and to face a new dawn. You cannot make progress by hanging on tightly to the very things that are holding you back. So, confront your fears head on, and the will flee from you.

Bat is there to help you see in the darkness and to find your way to a new understanding.

Key indicator: Ability to face your fears.

BEAR

The bear is an animal that hibernates in caves to get away from the outside environment. So as a power animal, it indicates that you have to search within to fulfil your hopes and aspirations, or to find solutions to your problems. Bear is concerned with the reaching of goals. Just as a bear withdraws from the outside world when it hibernates, so should you withdraw from your entanglements and seek refuge within – in the silence where the power of knowing is, and where the answers to your needs, and the harmony you seek, lie hidden.

Bear also stresses the importance of the dreamtime – the time to nurture your dreams and aspirations in a quiet periods, and to seek ways to 'own' them so they can become practical realities.

Bear is the power of the meditative state. So if you have Bear as a power animal ask it to help you find the centre of your being – the place of perfect balance and harmony – and make sure that time for inner looking becomes part of your daily routine.

Key indicator: Ability to draw strength from within.

BEAVER

Beaver is the construction worker of the animal world and its dam-building methods characterize its industriousness and productivity. As a power animal, Beaver stresses the power of work, and especially of teamwork, to accomplish what is necessary and obtain a sense of achievement.

Beaver as a power animal can help you to develop more harmonious relationships with others, and acquire a sense of involvement in any project. Beaver's practice of providing alternative ways of entering and leaving its home is a reminder that there is more than one way of solving your problems. Beaver is also cautioning you to protect what you have achieved or acquired through your own efforts.

If you are currently engaged in any creative endeavour. Beaver is encouraging you to put your ideas into practice. It is not enough to be a dreamer: you need to be a doer if you want your dreams to become practical realities.

Be constructive in all your endeavours, and look for ways of providing alternatives.

Key indicator: Ability to be persistent.

BUFFALO

The buffalo was the most sacred of all animals to the American Indian because it gave entirely of itself providing not only food, but also materials for clothing, housing, cooking utensils and equipment, and weapons. As a power animal Buffalo is thus concerned with provision and abundance, with sustenance and sharing. It stresses the importance of being prepared to share one's energies with others, and to recognize other people's needs.

Buffalo is also symbolic of Wakan-Tanka – the Great Spirit in manifestation, who was also referred to as the Great Everything – and is a reminder that whatever talents and abilities we may have they all derive from the source of the Great Provider. So Buffalo as a power animal serves as a reminder that everything we possess is but temporary, and that true happiness can never be attained alone; it comes through sharing what one has, and what one is, with others.

Key indicator: Ability to be sharing and caring.

BUTTERFLY

Tribal shamans regarded the butterfly as the keeper and protector of places of power, or power spots in Nature. No negative energies were experienced where there were butterflies, so their presence indicated a place of power free from negative influences.

The butterfly is an insect that transforms itself from an egg, to a larva, to a caterpiller, and then to a flying creature. As power animal Butterfly is emphasizing the importance of transformation in the continuous process of development and spiritual evolution. It is teaching the significance by enjoying the journey of life, and how you should not be consumed by 'goals'. A butterfly lives for only three days, so it emphasizes the need to enjoy the Now.

Butterfly stresses the importance of freedom from self-imposed constraints and the necessity for clarity of mind so that you can view problems and difficulties from a wider perspective.

Butterfly is a power animal that can help you to accept the pain of change in leaving behind old concepts and attitudes, and to have the courage to launch out on wings of hope to new situations and fresh challenges.

Key indicator: Ability to accept change.

COUGAR

Cougar is the mountain lion of western North America, Mexico, and Central and South America, and is also known as the puma. It has a handsome, cat-like face and a smooth and graceful body, with tawny-tan and grey colouration. As a power animal, Cougar encourages you to take charge of any troubling situation and to use your powers of leadership to influence events. It urges you to overcome your uncertainty and aloofness by accepting personal responsibility, and thus generate positive action.

Cougar provides strength, determination and foresight, and an assurance that right action leads to right results. It is endeavouring to show you how to be your own leader.

Key indicator: Ability to take responsibility.

COYOTE

The coyote is the North American equivalent of the jackal. The American Indian regarded the animal as a joker because of its highly amusing antics and habit of appearing to ignore the obvious. As a power animal, Coyote will teach you more about yourself and will help you to learn from your own mistakes. It can help you to smile at your own acts of foolishness, and not to take everything so painfully seriously. Coyote is concerned with breaking down the ego which is blocking your spiritual progress, and 'tricking' you into things you may find difficult, but which are necessary for your development.

Coyote encourages you to recognize that the mess you are in is largely your own fault. Ask Coyote to help you to look beneath the surface of the situation, and to see the course of your own actions from a different perspective. When you can stop blaming others, blaming circumstances, blaming fate or bad luck, Coyote will have taught you the lesson of that experience. Then, see the humorous side and laugh at your mistakes.

Coyote will continue to dog you if you persist in making the same mistake again!

Key indicator: Ability to recognize your own mistakes.

CRANE

The crane was revered by shamans of old and regarded as the keeper of secrets and of hidden knowledge. In some legends the Creator god was described as having long legs with which to stride over the primeval swamps. In Scandinavia, the crane was associated with Odin, to whom the living ciphers of the universe were revealed in the form of the Runes. Shamans of ancient Britain and Northern Europe had a 'medicine' bag made from the skin of the crane which was sometimes called a 'crane bag'. It was a round patch, tied with a drawstring containing Runes or other power objects.

Cranes and herons were said to be the first birds to greet the dawn, and in Scandinavia nesting comes were considered to be a protection against fire. Significantly the East is the direction of elemental Fire on the Medicine Wheel, and is related to spiritual enlightenment.

The crane or stork was associated with birth and new-born babies, because in olden times it was related to a goddess of fertility who was said to guide incarnating human spirits into the Middle World. Shamans considered the crane to be sacred to both god and goddess.

Since shamans regarded the crane as a guide to the Under-world – the realm of the Unconscious and of the Body Self – and it was so closely associated with the ciphers of the mysteries of Creation, there is a clear indication here that if you make the effort you will be able to reach your own hidden depths, and an understanding of the Runes.

Key indicator: Ability to look more deeply.

CROW

The shamanic ability to be 'shape shifters' – to perform magikal acts of bringing about desired changes in accordance with the will – was sometimes referred to by Indians as 'Crow medicine', for Crow helps to change the future.

Crow, as a proper animal, is urging you to let the past be your teacher. You cannot change it, but you can look into it and recognize those beliefs that have caused you suffering, so that you can now discard them. The present is the only true reality, for it is in the Now that the Future is created and fashioned. Change your thoughts and you change your future. Crow urges you to make more effective use of the present moment, and let the future be an inspiration.

Crow also signifies the need to find proper balance between ideals and practical reality, and reveals the ability to create the kind of future you want – if you apply your will to it.

Key indicator: Ability to find balance.

DEER

As a power animal, Deer stresses that there are other ways than force, and shows that there is power in the gentle word and touch, and that strength comes through caring.

You are confronted by those whose attitudes cause you pain and sorrow, and sometimes even fear. But it is they who are the wounded ones, and whoever tries to help them will only make matters worse. To soothe them you must touch their hearts with the healing balm of the gentle spirit and the embrace of kindliness.

Deer teaches the need for compassion and kindness towards others and yourself. Don't drive yourself so harshly! Be gentle with yourself, and you will cease to project your fears onto others. Deer is a power animal that is directing you towards a serenity of heart, mind and spirit.

Key indicator: Ability to be gentle with yourself.

DOLPHIN

The dolphin is a beautiful, gregarious mammal with a beaked mouth, and is found in all the oceans of the world. In American Indian cosmology, Dolphin is the Keeper of the Sacred Breath which contains the prana/mana life force, which is the essence of the Spirit. As a power animal, therefore, Dolphin is associated with the rhythm of energy within Nature and within your own body, and with revitalization.

Dolphin is symbolic of breath. By changing the rhythm of our breathing we can tune into other living things in the universe. This is why rhythmic breathing is so important.

Dolphin is concerned also with communication which, again, involves pattern and rhythm, and especially with sonics and with sonic harmonization. It is also associated with dreams and dreaming, and indicates that you should explore the oceans of your own dreamtime and examine carefully what you see there. Dolphin will help you to decipher their meaning.

Key indicator: Ability to re-vitalize

DRAGON

The dragon is a mythical animal which is usually presented as a giant, bat-winged, lizard-like creature with a scaly body and a forked tail. Scriptural literalists associated the dragon with the devil and evil, but in ancient times the dragon was regarded by most cultures as a benificent dweller of the inner Earth – of caves and lakes.

The word 'dragon' is derived from a Greek word meaning 'snake', which indicates that the creature was more like a serpent. The word also means 'to see', and the dragon is often depicted as having a searching gaze, which is actually one of its characteristics. The Chinese considered the dragon as a benevolent influence. An Azure Dragon was the 'keeper' of the eastern 'palace' in Chinese cosmology, and linked with the powers of the rising Sun, the Spring season and wood, indicating an association with new beginnings and growth. It is also one of the twelve cyclical animals in Chinese astrology in which it is associated with strength and fearlessness, with energy and health, and with prosperity and success. In British and European mythology it exemplified elemental Earth power and the vitality of the land.

So, far from being hated or feared, the dragon of antiquity was revered. Christian missionaries turned it, along with benevolent 'deities', into a servant of evil and a symbol of malevolent forces being conquered by 'saints'.

There is no need to fear a Dragon that appears as a power animal. After all, the dragon was often a symbol of wealth in ancient times. However, shamanically this prosperity may be of spiritual rather than material riches, because the dragon was regarded as the guardian of treasure that lay hidden deep in the unconscious and was hard to obtain. The dragon is making you aware that it is 'there'. Dragon is also depicted as breathing flames, but this serpent fire is the 'electrical' energy in the chakra 'cave' at the base of the spine which rises up when the Higher mind has been aroused. In other words, dragon is a sign of initiation!

Key indicator: Ability to find what you are seeking.

EAGLE

Eagle helps you to see beyond the mundane levels of visible existence, for Eagle as a power animal is your connection with your soul Self – your High Self. Eagle can help you to reach for the sky whilst still keeping your feet firmly on the ground, and thus combine lofty ideals with practical reality. Eagle can show you that principles and actions are equally expressions of the spirit.

In American Indian cosmology the eagle 'flies closest to the sun', meaning the illuminating light of the Great Spirit. Therefore, Eagle as a power animal brings enlightenment, which is a sudden flash of illumination, of seeing into spiritual truths which hitherto were obscured or unknown.

Key indicator: Ability to see the big picture

ELK

Elk stresses friendship and co-operation – the sense of unity that comes from belonging to a group or community. It emphasizes the need to establish relationships. If you are engaged in some kind of competitive activity, whether in your working life or in a personal relationship, you may feel threatened and under pressure. You need some equilibrium. Elk shows the value of friendships and of sharing your interests and experiences with others.

Elk stresses the importance of finding time for refreshment and reflection, and of renewing one's strength. Elk has to do with stamina and the need to go to those of the same gender for support.

Key indicator: Ability to renew and hold firm.

FOX

Fox is associated with cunning, primarily because of its ability to observe the movements of others without being seen. As a power animal, Fox stresses the power of adaptability and integration coupled with the qualities of quick-thinking and decisiveness when the time is ripe.

Power animals always express the positive aspects of the characteristics they share with their physical counterparts, and Fox is no exception. Fox as a power animal teaches not the cunning of deceitfulness, but the kenning of discretion; not the wilyness of being sly, but the willingness of being unobtrusive. It also stresses the importance of waiting patiently for the appropriate opportunity to make your move.

It is possible that your principal problems derive from your desire to prove yourself, and to make your presence felt. if you are feeling threatened, or the victim of controversy and criticism, or envy and jealousy, you are in need of Fox's help in becoming less noticeable and in achieving your aims unheeded and unimpeded by others.

Key indicator: Ability to be discreet.

FROG

Frog is a symbol of shamanism. It teaches how to 'jump' from one level to another – from materialism to spirituality, and from one teaching to another, and to find the connection between them.

The frog emerges at adulthood from a water environment (world of fluidity) to that of Earth (solidity and security). As a power animal, Frog can help you to acclimatize to a new way of life or to just a new viewpoint. Its power is in harmonizing you with any new situation. Frog also has to do with replenishment – the nurturing of the self – with taking care of yourself. So it can help you to get rid of any negativity and to replenish you mind and spirit.

Water is associated with absorption and diffusement, and Frog can help you to wash away ideas and impressions that might be impeding your development. Frog can help you to take the plunge – to have the courage to set out on a new endeavour and to accept the new way of life that goes with it.

Key indicator: Ability to adapt.

GRIFFIN

The griffin is a mythological hybrid monster which has the head and wings of an eagle, the body of a lion, and the tail of a serpent, so it combines the qualities of all these animals. Griffin is essentially a guardian and protector; this quality was recognized in its use as an heraldic figure on coats-of-arms in English and European history. The griffin was the private seal of Edward III who was King of England 1327–77. He planned the union between England and Scotland, and through his mother claimed the throne of France, thus starting the Hundred Years' War.

The griffin was associated with nobility and rulership, and so as a power animal is concerned with taking control over situations, while maintaining certain principles. Griffin is concerned with seeing beyond the obvious and of acting with both strength and determination, discretion and justness.

Key indicator: Ability to choose wisely.

HARE

The hare is a very elusive creature with an uncanny perception of its surroundings. In Celtic mythology the hare was regarded as an Otherworld guide and as the bringer of hidden teachings and intuitive messages.

Hare is one of the few animals to venture far afield during a full moon. It can see better by the moon's light, and therefore the ancient Celts associated it with the Goddess and made it a taboo animal which could only be hunted at certain times. Hares are not timid creatures like rabbits (with which they are usually confused).

It was the hare that was associated with 'bunny eggs', because it had no easily indentified nesting place. Its young appear almost fully grown, as if from nowhere.

As a power animal, Hare is associated with the unconscious mind.

Key indicator: Ability to act intuitively.

HAWK

As a power animal, Hawk 'awakens' not only the memory, but also the elements and the kingdoms, and it teaches you to look. Hawk can help you to be more observant, and to see ways out of a difficult situation. It encourages you to examine life from a higher perspective so you can identify new opportunities, as well as hazards that might block your progress.

Hawk also encourages you to look more closely at your everyday life, and especially for 'messages' that lie hidden in ordinary happenings. Messages of the spirit are often close at hand but obscured by the obvious.

Should you hear the shrill cry of the hawk during a shamanic journey, it may be a warning to beware of an impending event that may force you off balance, or it may be a call to be bold and decisive at the arrival of an unexpected opportunity. In any event, Hawk encourages you to follow the dictates of the heart.

Key indicator: Ability to be more observant.

HORSE

Perhaps more than any other animal, the horse has been humanity's closest partner in the animal kingdom. In ordinary reality it has carried its rider over distances and made communication possible. It has helped to shift heavy loads, and in the tilling of the soil. In non-ordinary reality the horse has carried the shamanic journeyer to communicate at other realms of existence, to shifts of consciousness, and to till the soil of deeper levels of the mind.

American Indians honoured the horse as a sacred animal. In Britain and Northern Europe, magikal fraternities once practised both the natural and supernatural powers associated with the cult of the horse.

As a power animal, Horse is primarily a message carrier and is often concerned with traversing 'gateways'. It is associated with the power and responsibility that comes from exercising authority, and the wisdom required to use it in a balanced way. On an emotional level, Horse is connected with the need for compassionate understanding.

Horse is related especially with the power of knowledge and wisdom, and with communication and sharing.

Key indicator: Ability to communicate.

HUMMINGBIRD

The hummingbird is a magnificent little creature that, unlike any other bird, can fly in any direction and even hover. Its long beak enables it to draw succulent nectar from every variety of flower. Its movement from one flower to another is a dance of delight, and its singing is a melody of ecstacy.

In American Indian folk stories, the hummingbird is associated with love and with joy. Its appearance as a power animal is indicative of the sheer delight of living, and of living the bliss of loving. It implies an ability to see beauty in everything and it is concerned with bringing out the best in people and the good in every situation.

Hummingbird embraces the highest principles and brings the magic of the spiritual realm into earthly activities. Hummingbird can help you to make the process of living a Dance of Beauty.

Key indicator: Ability to get to the essence of things.

LION

The lion has long been a symbol of imperial power and kingly wisdom, and has figured prominently in myths and legends and in religious and secular history. In all these areas the heart of the lion has been emphasized. As a power animal, the Lion is especially concerned with the heart and with bringing out the best in you, so welcome it as a true friend.

Among Lion's many qualities is its recuperative powers. The power to become quickly re-energized after physical depletion; the ability to recover from the trough of adversity; to heal the wounds of emotional hurts; these are all areas in which Lion may be of practical value. Lion is also symbolic of sexual energy, and the 'taming of the lion' in many ancient stories is an allegory of controlling sexual energy.

As a power animal Lion brings warmth, sincerity and self-assurance.

Key indicator: Ability to develop self-esteem.

LIZARD

The lizard is a creature found in shady areas during the heat of the day, and is symbolic of the shadowy side of reality – the plane where what is coming into manifestation is being fashioned. This plane is sometimes referred to as the 'dreamworld' – the astral plane of constantly changing patterns and shapes. Lizard is concerned with your dreams of the future and of formulating what you want to become physical realities.

Lizard is thus connected with your subconscious mind, and your hopes and fears. It can help you to identify those recurrent problems that follow you around like your shadow; they must be confronted before they will depart from you. Your aspirations must have emotion breathed into them to make them manifest.

Next time you encounter Lizard on a shamanic journey, look carefully behind you. Record your observations in a log and note especially any symbols and signs so that you can identify those that are recurring. Ask Lizard to help you to understand what you see. Keep a dream log, too, so you can become aware of what is occurring both in your dream state and your shamanic state of consciousness.

Key indicator: Ability to 'ground' your aspirations.

LYNX

The lynx is a large, feline creature with a pretty and smiling face. Some shamans describe it as a 'knowing' smile, and one might compare it with the self-satisfied smile of someone who knows something you don't.

In some American Indian mystical traditions, the lynx is regarded as the 'Keeper of Secrets' and the knower of that which is hidden. So Lynx is associated with the deeper truths and with clairvoyant and divinatory skills.

As a power animal, Lynx can teach you things you don't know – or have forgotten – about yourself. Lynx is a silent animal and emphasizes the necessity of going into the silence in order to understand 'hidden' knowledge and to obtain facets of ancient wisdom.

Watch Lynx's antics carefully on your shamanic journey, for it will rarely, if ever, speak. Watch where it is leading you to and from. As you record your impressions later, consider what thoughts and mental pictures come into mind. They may not appear to have any relevance at first, but that may be Lynx's way of imparting hidden knowledge to you.

Lynx may lead you to things that are lost or hidden, or to recall a forgotten incident which has relevance to your life now. It may be the whereabouts of a missing object, or a person with whom you have lost contact. Lynx may encourage you to consult an oracle for advice or to seek some means of divining the future.

Key indicator: Ability to listen to the silence.

MOUSE

Mouse is an animal with a highly sensitive sense of touch through its whiskers. Since it is a source of food for many animals it has a keen sense of danger too.

In American Indian medicine traditions, Mouse is associated with the ability to examine things in detail at close quarters. So Mouse, as a power animal, encourages you to pay more attention to detail and examine the 'small print' of what comes before you. Mouse also urges you to examine the details of your life more closely, and not to disregard the 'little' things, for they are all components of your life and teachers for your spiritual progress. Mouse tells you not to ignore the obvious because that which you are seeking may be right in front of your eyes.

Mouse also puts you on the alert. Things and people aren't always what they appear. Be careful not to be trapped into situations that might be harmful to you, or be enticed by offers that appear· attractive but may contain hidden snags. Examine everything carefully.

Key indicator: Ability to see the fine detail.

OTTER

Otter is a playful, joyful animal that is very protective of its young and is at home on land or in water. As a power animal, Otter stresses the need for compassionate understanding, balanced judgement and generous sharing. Otter helps you not only to be willing to share the good things of your life with others, but also to find pleasure in other people's achievements and good fortune. If you are happy for others you will find more joy in your own life.

Otter is an antedote to worry and anxiety. It emphasizes how important it is not to concern yourself too intensely with acquiring more material 'goodies' or advancing your position career-wise. Otter encourages you to find satisfaction in what you have and to enjoy life rather than to merely tolerate it.

Key indicator: Ability to enjoy.

OWL

Owl is a creature of the night and has been symbolically associated with wisdom because it can see what others cannot. It is the only bird that flies in total silence.

As a power animal, Owl encourages you to develop your intuitive abilities and inner senses, and to seek the knowledge that is hidden from most people. Owl is a protector and will help you to discern more readily the motives and intentions of others, especially those who may attempt to deceive you or take advantage of you in some way. Owl also helps you to recognize that there is a dark side to your nature that should not be ignored or repressed. You need to see that it is there so you can come to terms with it.

Owl is symbolic of discernment and the need to look out for deception.

Key indicator: Ability to understand.

PORCUPINE

I had not come across anyone who had experience of Porcupine as a power animal until it appeared in one of my own journeys. It has appeared periodically since, and has become an important influence in my life. I mistook it at first, for a hedgehog, except that it was much bigger. It was remarkably playful, and I only recognized it as a porcupine when I felt that its quills were not at all prickly.

What Porcupine taught me was the value of not taking life too seriously. Life is not intended as something to be suffered and endured, but should be appreciated and enjoyed. Porcupine showed me that adults need to rediscover the joy of the child to whom life is an adventure of pleasurable discovery.

Porcupine may not be among the most attractive of animals, but its child-like curiosity can be quite endearing. It is a humble animal which can teach us not only the need for humility but also the strength of joy it can impart.

Key indicator: Ability to find strength in humility.

RABBIT

Rabbit as a power animal is concerned with fears and anxieties. Rabbit provides the ability to know that something is wrong. You may have been attracted to Rabbit because you are the kind of person who hopes for the best, but fears the worst. Rabbit is showing you that it is not a matter of pretending such fears do not exist, or even of trying to resist them. You need to burrow down to bring them to the surface and then get rid of them – give them to the universe.

One way of revealing them is to write them down on a piece of paper, then conduct a little fire ceremony and set light to the paper. You can see your fears and anxieties vanish into the universe before your very eyes. Let the ashes of the burning paper fall into a small metal container or bowl. Then go outdoors, dig a small hole in the ground and bury them. This symbolic act shows that your worries no longer have a place in your life. Nearly all your fears are imaginary; now they are buried you can have faith in the future.

Rabbit, you see, can turn the weakness of fear into the strength of faith if you will accept its challenge.

Key indicator: Ability to know when something is wrong for you.

RAVEN

Because of its blackness, Raven has, in western cultures, been considered an omen of ill-fortune and associated with dark deeds. But in American Indian medicine traditions, light comes out of darkness, and black is associated with the Void – the source of all energy – Raven its messenger. That is why it is associated with magik and with fate, for it is a messenger of that which is to come.

Raven heralds the need to make dramatic changes in your attitudes and in the way you perceive things. Raven is encouraging you to put some real 'magik' into your life – to expect the unexpected, to prepare for plenitude. Disperse that negative attitude that has been holding you back for so long, replace it with the zest and excitement of 'alive-ness'. Feel good about being alive.

Raven is the courier of the energy-flow that brings about changes and creates new realities. In American Indian mystical traditions, Raven was the Guardian of Ceremonial Magik and Absent Healing. It therefore represented the power that carried the 'message' or intention of the ceremony to its destination, and thus brought about is manifestation.

Key indicator: Ability to foresee the need to change.

REINDEER

The reindeer is a species of caribou, whose habitat is in the northern climates of Alaska, Canada, Greenland, Scandinavia, Lappland and Russia. Reindeer provide milk, meat and hides. It is the 'horse' of the north, able to carry large loads and draw sledges. Some reindeer migrate hundreds of miles from their breeding grounds to their summer haunts, following the trails of their ancestors.

The reindeer figures in the folk tales and legends of northern peoples, and is the animal that transports the mythical Santa Claus, the bearer of gifts and joyfulness.

As a power animal, Reindeer is associated with the attributes of the North – clarity of mind, purity of intent, and rebirth and renewal. It is a bringer of the gifts of knowledge and wisdom from the trails of one's own ancestry. It signifies the joy of knowing and sharing, and of close relationships. It implies a need to migrate into the past to gain sustenance from ancient trails.

Key indicator: Ability to give.

SALMON

Salmon is able to swim against the strongest currents and is the master of water. It can help to show you how to tackle the water of emotions, heal your emotional hurts, and move through life without resistance.

As a power animal, Salmon is associated with longevity and with growing old gracefully, it can also help you to get in touch with and benefit from your own ancestral lineage and past life recall.

Key indicator: Ability to master the emotions.

SNAKE

Snake is a reptile that is able to shed its skin and live through a traumatic life-death-rebirth experience. So as a power animal Snake is associated with continuity of life and with transmutation from one experience to another, and from one level of existence to another.

Snake teaches you to recognize that you are an eternal being experiencing mortality, you are constantly shedding anything that has served its purpose, in favour of something which is of greater value.

Snake has transformational ability and supplies the power to use Fire energy in a correct way.

Key indicator: Ability to let go of what has served its purpose.

SQUIRREL

One thing you can be certain of in an uncertain world is the inevitability of change. So be adaptable and come into harmony with the cycles of change. That is part of the message of Squirrel as a power animal. Squirrel emphasizes the importance of planning ahead and of setting aside things for future needs. It means being prepared for changes, and even adversities, and being ready to respond to them positively.

Squirrel teaches you always to have something in reserve – not in the sense of being a hoarder, or a miser, but in a balanced way, setting aside for future needs even though it may not be required later.

Perhaps you have been living entirely on a day-to-day basis. Squirrel is reminding you to be more thrifty with your time and with your energy.

Key indicator: Ability to look ahead.

SWAN

The swan is, perhaps, the most regal and graceful of birds, yet it develops from a cygnet which is sometimes described as an ugly duckling. As a power animal, Swan is a symbol of dreams in which knowledge is imparted to further one's progress in spiritual evolution and to become a creation of great beauty.

So Swan is a helper in a transformational process and teaches the need to accept change with grace.

Key indicator: Ability to accept gracefully.

TURTLE

In Native American mythology, Turtle represented the Earth, the mother from whose substance the bodies of all creatures living on Earth were formed, and the nurturing Force that provides an opportunity for the human spirit to evolve.

As a power animal, Turtle teaches the need for protection. Although you should find expression for the creative sources within, and allow your thoughts to reach up to 'heavenly' things, it is essential to stay well grounded and to be connected to the power of the Earth. In other words, you must keep your feet on the ground of practicality. Turtle also stresses the need to keep the physical body in balance, and to remember that this is the vehicle through which we experience life on Earth.

Turtle teaches the wisdom of aligning yourself the cyclic flow of life, and demonstrates that the fastest way is not necessarily the best, for it takes time for ideas to develop properly.

Turtle indicates Earth harmony, and draws you to all that is whole and good and abundant.

Key indicator: Ability to make progress surely.

UNICORN

The unicorn is a hybrid mythical animal with the body of a sleek white horse, the legs of an antelope, and the tail of a lion, so it incorporates the attributes of all these creatures. In addition it possesses a most magikal asset – a single horn which grows out of its head – which is a symbol of supreme magikal power. Catch your unicorn and whatever you wish is yours! The base of the horn is usually pure white, the middle portion is gold and black, and the sharp tip is a vivid crimson.

According to legend, the unicorn is so elusive it can be caught only by a virgin maiden. This implies that the very essense of one's being cannot be captured by any physical means but only by innocent receptiveness – in other words, by the feminine side of our nature, whichever our sex. It is about the union of the Human Self and the Hidden Self; the creativity of making something of your life every single day, rather than just 'passing time'.

As a power animal, then, Unicorn has great significance for it is concerned with the inner world of the mind and of the imagination, and their relationship with both physical and spiritual reality.

Key indicator: Ability to make your dream come true.

WEASEL

Weasel has an acute sense of hearing and ability to see beneath the surface. As a power animal, Weasel helps you to develop your inner hearing so that you can listen to your inner voice, and to heighten your perception so you can see beneath the words and actions of others and ascertain their true motives and intentions.

Weasel is a help in determining the reasons why something is so when the reason may not be obvious. So ask Weasel for help in those areas of life which are confusing or worrying, and ask for answers to why you feel as you do about a particular situation.

Key indicator: Ability to see beneath the surface.

WHALE

Whale figures in the folklore of all cultures and is a creature of great antiquity. In Amerindian legends the whale is associated with the time before the sea swallowed up whole continents in a great world-wide catastrophe. It is therefore regarded as the carrier of ancient knowledge.

Whale as a power animal is concerned with bringing messages out of the depths of your being – out of ancestral memories that lie deep within you in your DNA code. The answers to many of life's greatest perplexities lie hidden there, as well as the records of your own past and the indications of your own destiny. Whale can help you to go deep down into the oceans of Time and discover and understand the ancient wisdom.

Whale can also help you to find your own unique sound pattern and your own power song that can link you to the 'heartbeat' of the universe. Whale has a power song of its own which Silver Bear told me 'informs Sirius what Earth children are doing'!

Key indicator: Ability to obtain wisdom from the past.

WINGED HORSE

The winged horse is a mythical animal – a magnificent creature that can gallop through the air and convey its rider into other dimensions. It is symbolic of inspiration which seems to come from another 'world' because it embraces ideas that have not been worked at and reasoned into existence. A winged horse also symbolizes the soul's immortality, and ability to function both in the physical world of matter and in the invisible realm of the spirit.

The winged horse has figured in the myths and legends of all cultures. Among the northern peoples it was Sleipner, the magikal eight-legged horse which conveyed the shaman 'deity' Odin to Other-worlds. Its teeth were inscribed with the Runes, indicating that it carried the language of the Cosmos in its mouth.

As a power animal the Winged Horse enables you to soar to spiritual heights, and to experience that which is beyond the power of the intellect. Should Winged Horse appear, get on its back and let it carry you 'beyond the stars'.

Key indicator: Ability to scale the heights.

WOLF

In American Indian cosmology, wolf is not regarded as a lethal animal but as a teacher and pathfinder – one who leads the way. The wolf has highly developed senses: its nose, for instance, is a hundred times more sensitive than the human's. It can sense the difference between real and imagined dangers.

The confrontation of Wolf as a power animal is an indication of being taken to meet your Inner Teacher and to receive direct, personal teaching. Wolf will reveal to you that anyone and anything can be a teacher. You can learn from trees, plants, animals, birds, rocks and stones, and even from the wind and the rain. You just need to be alert and learn to listen.

Wolf thus indicates a coming forth of knowledge that is beneath the level of consciousness and within the unconscious.

Key indicator: Ability to extend the senses.

THE POWER DANCE

After 'acquiring' a power animal during a shamanic journey shamans sometimes use a technique called the Power Dance to bring the energy to the surface. In a power dance the shaman endeavours not only to sense the energy-force of the power animal with which he has been dealing in non-ordinary reality, but to flow and move with it and become one with it in ordinary reality. Such movements constitute the 'dance'. In endeavouring to identify with the energy in this way and to stimulate the movements of the physical creature with which the power animal has similarities, even perhaps to mimic animal sounds or calls, the shaman comes into harmony with it.

The power dance is an expression in ordinary consciousness of the existence of a source of power that lies in an altered state of consciousness. In other words, the dancer is in a borderline state, a 'twilight' condition where the two dimensions meet. For this reason it is best to squint the eyes while moving around to attain 'twilight' sight and bring the inner eyes into play, to see what is hidden from physical view.

Relax your body so that you can move easily in any direction. Move around to the rhythm of a drum (if you are working with other people), or just use a rattle if you are on your own. Use a bouncy step, rattling as you go, with your feet flat on the floor so you are firmly in contact with the ground. Shift your weight from one foot to the other, expressing the 'mood' of the energies with your whole body and not just with the mind. Release your inhibitions and let yourself go – or rather, flow.

You may feel a desire to simulate the movements of the animal – to prance like a horse, stalk like a lion, glide like a hawk, leap like a monkey, run like a deer, and so on. Let yourself move in whatever way the animal dictates. It is an aspect of the animalistic side of your nature seeking expression in a benevolent way. The power dance is thus more than a primitive demonstration of animal movement, but is the uninhibited expression of energy surfacing from subconscious and unconscious depths so that it can be recognized and used.

For the purpose of encountering a power animal on a shamanic journey, and of recognizing its essential characteristics, is not simply for the satisfaction of the experience. It is so that energy potential can be put to use. The power dance is a means of getting the 'feel' of it and of identifying with it so that one is better able to work with it

INTEGRATION AND EMBODIMENT

A Power Dance is a method of demonstrating willing acceptance of an energy-pattern that has been retrieved on a shamanic journey. This power of ability needs to be integrated lovingly – that is, it requires to be *desired* in order that it can be embodied to become pat of one's physical and mental reality.

It requires an acceptance that it is *there* and an affirmation that it is *yours*. This process of integration and embodiment can be attained simply by meditating upon it whilst rattling or drumming.

CHAPTER NINE

Guides, Teachers and Guardians

IN ADDITION TO POWER ANIMALS, totems and power objects, shamanists have inner teachers who instruct them, give counsel, and protect them. Inner guides and teachers usually appear in human form during shamanic journeys, some as archetypal figures such as wise old men, wildmen of the forest, medieval ladies, or even as children or fairies. Guardians can present themselves in human and non-human forms.

Shamanic guides and teachers are not imaginary figures 'manufactured' in the mind and existing only as illusions. They are images of another reality which co-exists with the ordinary world of our waking consciousness. Let me attempt to define the difference between a shamanic guide and an inner teacher.

A guide is an energy-pattern that supplies information vital to your growth and development. It operates beyond the range of ordinary physical perception. Any visual impression we receive comes from the Hidden Self via the subconscious mind, in a form that both the Hidden Self and the Human Self's conscious mind can each recognize.

A guardian is a protective influence who assists the shaman in accomplishing his tasks, and who guards him from harm both during spirit journeys to Other-worlds and during physical activities. A guardian is the equivalent of what religious people might call a 'guardian angel'. It is permanently with you, always seeking to protect you from harm whether the danger is physical, emotional, mental, or spiritual, and advising you through what is sometimes referred to as 'the voice of conscience'. Power animals, which I discussed in Chapter 8, serve as guides, helpers and guardians, and suppliers of the energies needed for particular tasks.

An inner teacher usually appears in human form during shamanic journeys. Sometimes, however, in order to make a teaching clear it may appear in animal form to impress a point in a very personal teaching. These are not imaginary figures manufactured in the mind, but images of another reality which co-exists with the ordinary world of our waking consciousness.

One of the purposes of your inner teacher is to supply information which is vital to your development. It functions beyond the range of ordinary physical perception. Any visual impressions you might receive come from this hidden source via the subconscious mind in a form that both the inner teacher and your conscious mind can recognize.

The inner teacher acts also as a guide in your ordinary everyday life giving you nudges by way of intuition or hunches. If you listen to these very closely your life can take a much smoother route, particularly in the choice of partners and in handling relationships. Your inner teacher has sought to protect you all your life, trying to guard you from harm and from dangers whether they be physical, emotional, mental or spiritual, 'speaking' to you through your intuition, hunches, or what you might have thought as your 'conscience'.

The inner teacher has evolved through a human life in a connection with your Spirit and in that life had an inner teacher of its own that was connected with its spirit which is now your Spirit. So your inner teacher has experienced life and learned from those experiences. It is now experiencing spiritual evolution as a guide whose own progress is linked with yours. It is your ally. Its other purpose is to show you the way to *your* Spirit, to *your* place of ecstacy, *your* source of all that is.

However, it is with the conscious Human Self that you immediately identify, the 'self' of your material existence with its likes and dislikes. It is a 'self' that is rarely satisfied, ever making comparisons, constantly making judgements, egotistical, full of expectations, and continually seeking its own advantage.

The High Self is your individual link with divinity because it is closer to the Ultimate Source of All That Is. It is concerned with your ultimate good and provides opportunities to further your spiritual development. It makes no demands on you, enforces no action and does not control you like a puppet. This is because your free will – the freedom to decide what to do and not to do and to learn from experience – is sacrosanct. Spiritual evolution can only take place through learning from the consequences of one's thoughts and actions. Because the High Self is located in the Nagual, it has an overview of your life at any time; it can see in all directions – Past, Present and immediate Future – and is able to perceive how all the 'pieces' of your life fit together, as in a jig-saw puzzle.

High Self qualities can be expressed through the Human Self. Unconditional love, for instance, is a feature of the High Self – that is, love given without the expectance of anything in return. Possessive and demanding love is not really love but the self-indulgence of the egotistical Human Self.

Actually, one of the greatest fallacies and tragedies of human history is that most people are led to believe that love comes from *outside* themselves – a quality that comes to them from someone else. That is why it is sought so hard. That is why it is sought so desperately. The truth is that love comes from *within* the very core of our being and seeks only to be shared. Its source is the High Self. For love is an activity of the Spirit, not just an exercise of the mind or body. When this discovery is made love can be released to flow freely from ourselves and back to ourselves.

Your High Self loves you totally, in spite of yourself. It cares about what happens to you and wants you to fulfil your life's purpose here and now. Your High Self is always for you, always supportive, always 'there', ever-present but rarely apparent. Indeed, most people are not even aware that they have a High Self, and are aware only of the personality self.

The High Self is itself developing toward greater perfection through the experiences – positive and negative, 'good' and 'bad' – of the Human Self. Part of a mortal's life on Earth is to establish a willful link between the Human Self, the Hidden Self, and the High Self. We need to bring the High Self into active participation with our Human Self in our everyday life. In doing so our relationship with 'divinity' is changed from an idea of nebulous 'heavenly' supernaturality to one of down-to-Earth practical reality, from that of being 'up There' to that of being 'down Here' in the Creation with us, closer than our heart. The Hidden Self is the pivotal link between the Soul, Mind and Body. The physical body is maintained in being by the Body Self for the purpose of making evolutionary development possible. That is why we are here – to thrive and to endure.

Any expectation that our life should be run for us by others – whether parents, teachers, spiritual leaders, the government, or even 'God' – is a frustration of that purpose. We need to come to a realization that we must accept responsibility for our own life. Part of that is an acceptance of what we are here to learn through experience. That responsibility is to the High Self and in response the High Self provides inner teaching and guidance.

The inner teacher, though in the realm of the spirit, is very practical, down-to-earth, and interested in your everyday life. It will sometimes prompt you into partnership, just for a while, with a physical teacher functioning in the realm of ordinary reality. A student of shamanism today may be receiving oral or written teaching from a shaman on the physical plane, and also esoteric knowledge from a teacher on the inner planes, both of whom are operating in partnership on a spiritual level. For instance this book, and my others in the Earth Quest series, has been written from knowledge obtained partly from oral instruction received from practising shamans, partly from my own experience and research, but also from inner-plane teaching. It is through an inner teacher that a shaman is empowered to tap a repository of ancient knowledge and wisdom. Indeed, shamans were historically guardians of the 'mysteries' of life because they were perceivers of the invisible and the hearers of 'unspoken' words. And this is one reason why the revival of shamanism is so important today, for it is not only a way of knowledge and creativity but a way of making contact with the divinity within. To the shamanist divinity is no remote stranger but a loving companion.

TEACHERS

Shamanic journeys to the Upper World – the mystic realm of the Soul – is a way of establishing contact with the High Self through teachers and guides that may be encountered there.

What do these teachers and guides look like? Sometimes a teacher appears as a man and sometimes as a woman, and sometimes as a man and woman together. This is because the High Self is a duality and has both masculine and feminine aspects. The Yin and Yang symbol is not only an expression of the duality principle inherent in Nature, but also of the High Self. It represents the High Self as male and female 'soul mates', united as one yet still retaining the individual attributes of gender.

HELPERS

Helpers provide assistance in shamanic work or supply the power or ability to perform certain functions. They usually appear in shamanic journeys in non-human forms – sometimes as fantasy figures but more often as animals, as trees and plants, or as rocks, stones or gems. These latter three carry a wealth of meaning if we know how to look. Images of the mineral kingdom can be drawn up from unconscious levels of the mind, and after a 'journey' may be considered in their three physical aspects of texture, shape and colour.

Texture: A smooth stone or rock has a gentle and soothing feeling, calming to the emotions and dispelling fears and anxieties. So a smooth stone encountered on a shamanic journey indicates the provision of comfort and support. A rough stone is one that has been weathered by experience and that embraces the wisdom of the ages. Sometimes it takes on the appearance of a weatherbeaten face; sometimes it may appear to have animal features. If it has a human 'face', ask yourself what emotion or quality it portrays and apply it to your own circumstance. If a rock or stone looks like an animal, it is likely to be portraying the attributes of that animal. So, again, relate those animal characteristics to your own situation.

Shape: A round stone suggests contentment through a willingness to be flexible and adaptable, whereas an oval stone indicates a need to seek change. Pyramid shapes are symbolic of intuitiveness and inner 'knowing', while four-sided rocks suggest dependability arising out of self-discipline and self-exertion. Five-sided rocks and stones indicate inventiveness and creativity, and those with six sides stress sincerity and decisiveness. A stone with a hole is protective and uplifting.

Colour: Reddish stones convey strength and vitality and the exertion of physical and emotional energy. Green is the colour of harmony and these stones are a reminder that love is the great bonding force. Yellow stones are concerned with the need for clarity in conveying thoughts and ideas. Blue and grey stones emphasize peace and serenity and are associated with devotion and duty. White stones convey purity of intent and purpose and highlight the need to give and to share and to be outward-looking. Black stones are to do with absorbing and receiving and of being inward-looking.

Gemstones encountered on shamanic journeys are also symbolic. Here are some clues:

Agate:	mental stimulation.
Amber:	growth and development.
Amethyst:	emotional help.
Crystal:	spiritual development.
Diamond:	prosperity.
Emerald:	development of inner vision.
Jade:	balanced judgement.
Jasper:	Earth wisdom.
Moonstone:	intuition and receptiveness.
Obsidian:	banishment.
Onyx:	practicalities.
Opal:	perception.
Rose quartz:	friendships.
Ruby:	loyalty.
Sapphire:	affluence.
Turquoise:	inner peace.

Sea-shells deal with career matters and coral is concerned with personal relationships.

Metals encountered on a shamanic journey can also be significant. *Gold*, for instance, is a great attracter, drawing all things to it and having a steadying influence. Gold emphasizes material affairs and the present. *Silver*, on the other hand, emphasizes spiritual values and links the past with the future. *Iron* has bonding qualities and is concerned with holding things together. *Copper* has to do with elimination and healing – with drawing out what is no longer needed and casting it off so it can do no harm. *Lodestone* is associated with magnetism and with the transmission of energy – of sending out as well as drawing in.

GUARDIANS

We have examined the help that can come from power animals, we have discussed teachers on the inner planes, and helpers from the mineral kingdom. Now let us turn to guardians in the plant kingdom – the trees and woodland plants which often figure in shamanic journeys. They are there to impart much knowledge and wisdom if we show a willingness to become attuned to them.

Trees can serve as guardians and guides because humans have an affinity with them, though many are ignorant of such a connection. Like trees, we began life as a seed which contained within it our individual potential. Like trees, we are nourished from the soil and by the Sun. Like trees, we grow and blossom in adulthood to provide shelter and protection for others. And like trees we, too, withstand the storms and traumas of life.

On the physical plane the primary purpose of trees is to guard and protect the Earth's environment. Without them the atmosphere would become polluted through an excess of carbon dioxide, ultimately contaminating the environment. On another level, trees are the imagery of protective forces, and also symbols of energy-power and of dormant potentials. This imagery surfaces from hidden depths of the subconscious and unconscious when an altered state of mind brings it to the attention of the consciousness.

As I have stated earlier, everything that transpires on a shamanic journey has significance. The sight of a particular species of tree or trees is no exception. Such images are 'messengers' with something of importance to convey. How can we unlock their meaning? Partly through understanding a tree's physical characteristics and applying them in human terms and partly through a further journey to seek a fuller explanation.

Here is a list of the attributes of trees and bushes that figure prominently in shamanic journeys. It should help the shamanic adventurer to arrive at a more meaningful understanding of the shamanic experience:

Alder: The alder is associated with transition and transformation, indicating that adversity contains within it the seeds of a new beginning. Alder imparts serenity and the power to avoid being swept away on emotional tides. It teaches the need for calmness and the strength that comes from taking an overview of a situation.

Ash: The ash provides a key to understanding the holistic nature of the universe and of realizing how the material and the spiritual are connected. It also shows how one's inner thoughts ultimately find expression in the outer world of physical manifestation. The ash tree indicates the need for a change of lifestyle to attain a right relationship with the Earth and to link the outer and inner worlds. Its special quality is resilience.

Apple: Shamans have associated the apple tree with making decisions and right choices, and with challenging options. The apple is protective and helpful in those areas of human activity in which talents and skills are required to be nurtured and developed through consistent care and persistent practice. It emphasizes concentration.

Beech: The beech tree is linked with the thirst for knowledge that nourishes the soul, and is a guardian of 'lost' wisdom and a door of access to it for those who quest for it with love in their hearts. It guards against repeating mistakes and helps in the establishment of a firm foundation for future action.

Fir: The fir tree is the plant kingdom's equivalent of the eagle. It is the protector of distant vision, enabling the likely outcome of present or intended actions to be foreseen and perspectives to be broadened. It is the tree of the visionary and of the seer.

Gorse: The gorse or furze bush is associated with purification and with replenishment. It is the protector of efforts to gather the skills and requisites necessary to attain that which is desired.

Hazel: The hazel's pliable branches provided shamans with dowsing tools, while wands and staffs come from its thicker branches. Hazel stresses the power of divination, the ability to discern Nature's subtle influences and the skill that is necessary to direct the will. It teaches the value of quiet contemplation regarding the direction of creative energies, and of self-sacrifice in taking care of the needs of others.

Heather: Since heather grows close to the ground it is associated with practicalities. It was considered 'lucky' because its soothing qualities enhanced the pleasantries of dreams and aspirations from which the future is fashioned by the subconscious. Heather guards the 'dream time' from negativities thus bringing a good future and good fortune.

Holly: Holly enhances the qualities of vigour and aggressiveness and stresses the need for direct action but with balanced judgment. It is the guardian of the moment, indicating the need to accept the reality of the present and to learn from it.

Honeysuckle: The entwining branches of the honeysuckle and the heady fragrance of its flowers were associated with sensuousness and eroticism and the gradual revealing of secrets. In some cultures it was a symbol of the labyrinth and the quest for secrets of the soul. So honeysuckle is concerned with finding a way to your own spiritual centre and enjoying the thrill of the experience. It guards from distractions.

Ivy: Ivy's energy is that of the wanderer so it is associated with travel and the exploration of unknown places. It is related to forward vision and with perceiving what is beyond that immediately to hand. It is a guardian of regeneration.

Oak: The oak's special qualities are strength and durability. It grows slowly but its development is sure, so it stresses the importance of patience and the fact that great things develop from small beginnings. It is the guardian of the power of inner achievement and stresses the need not to allow the limitations of logic-based systems of knowledge to smother hopes and aspirations.

Poplar: Wood from the poplar was once made into shields, indicating that the tree not only resists attack but strengthens the resolve in the face of difficulties. The poplar is a symbol of hope and an expression of encouragement in doing what the heart tells you is right. Its leaves whisper in the wind as if each leaf is conversing. So the poplar encourages you to whisper your silent thoughts and to express your feelings with gentleness.

Reed: The long, straight stalk of the reed was compared with the shaft of an arrow which the warrior/hunter needed to choose with great care if it was to be as true as the intentions. So reed teaches the importance of finding direction and having the intention clearly in mind; it also suggests inner strength with the need to bend and adjust to changes.

Silver birch: The silvery-white trunk of the silver birch symbolizes purity of intent and determination of spirit, and provides an indication that clarity of purpose is essential to the success of any shamanic mission. The silver birch strengthens and clarifies the image of what is desired, brings the intention into sharp focus, and guards the image from diffusion. Silver birch indicates beginnings and an upsurge of energy usually associated with things that are fresh and new.

Willow: The willow's pliable branches were used for basket weaving and for stockades and thatch supports. Thus it stresses the importance of the receptive and nurturing qualities, of drawing things together in proper balance, and of the need for protection and support. Willow teaches the need for adaptability and, in a world of changing values, of finding satisfaction in the process rather than the ultimate goal.

Yew: The yew is one of the longest-surviving trees — it can live for over a thousand years — so it is associated with longevity. It emphasizes continuity in the face of constant change, the need to regard death as an advisor and every change as but a transition to another beginning.

Before concluding this chapter let me stress that these descriptions are intended only as indications and not interpretations. They are offered as possible clues to an underlying meaning, and need to be considered not in objective isolation but in the context of what is seen and heard in the shamanic experience itself. These clues may then trigger a response that will enable you more quickly to arrive at a productive interpretation of your shamanic experience.

Once contact has been established with an Inner Teacher, you can consult him or her for advice or information by making a shamanic journey to the Upper World. On each occasion consider carefully the concern in your life for which you require help, but do not phrase your question in such a way that it invites a simple yes or no answer. Your Inner Teacher is not there to make decisions for you. You determine of your own actions and must take responsibility for them. A question to the Inner Teacher seeks guidance: the likely effect of a line of action, for instance, the best attitude to adopt to attain a particular aim, the lesson to be learned from a situation you are in, or how best to respond to an action that is affecting you.

Defining clearly the purpose of your mission is an essential part of the shamantic journeying experience. So focus your question by first writing it down and then amending it as you give it thoughtful attention until it is clear and precise. Then you will ensure a meaningful response each time.

CHAPTER TEN

Directionology

THE PHYSICAL HUMAN BODY is symmetrically designed so that we perceive the world around us in one of four directions – front or back, and left or right sides. These can be sub-divided to provide more precise locations. Everything around us is energy. The five physical senses enable us to respond to that energy, which is perceived as 'reality'. In fact it is not 'real' at all, but only what 'appears' to be.

In ancient cultures geographical direction and location had a bearing on the way individuals perceived life, and had a vital influence on decision-making. For instance, whether a girl should marry a particular suitor might have been decided by the implications indicated by the direction in which he lived in relation to her. The likely success of an enterprise might depend upon where the bearer of the proposition had come from, or on the direction in which one might have to travel in order to conclude an arrangement. The siting of entrances to tribal villages, and gateways to towns and cities, was significant, as were the positions of doors or openings to individual dwellings within a community. Even the qualities of the prevailing wind were thought to be influenced by the direction from which it blew.

The directions were linked to great Powers, intelligent influences whose powers could be harnessed. The directions could be charted on a circular 'map' – the Medicine Wheel or Circle of Power – which was a device that enabled one to come into alignment with these spiritual powers and absorb something of them.

The division of a circle into four parts could be made to correspond with the apparent movements of the Sun, and so with the periods of day – dawn, noon, dusk and midnight – and also with the seasons of the year. The division could be made in two ways: by lines running from the centre to the four cardinal points of North, South, East and West, or by lines connecting to the four non-cardinal directions of North-east, South-east, South-west and North-west. Together this eight-fold division resulted in a quarter facing its cardinal direction – so North runs from North-west to North-east, East from North-east to South-east, and so on. This eight-fold division also emphasized the Harmonic Law of Octaves which was fundamental to an understanding of the dynamics of the Cosmos as it affects human life.

When the Medicine Wheel is drawn as a two-dimensional chart, North is at the 'top'. The Cosmic Tree was similarly oriented with North considered as being 'in front' (or at the 'top' of a two-dimensional chart). One reason for this was that when darkness fell the North star was the first point of reference to establish direction, the pivotal point on which the entire universe appeared to turn. So for the shaman, seeking to find his way in that which was normally 'hidden', in the 'darkness' of the 'unknown', North was the obvious first point of reference from which to establish a position in space and time. Another reason is that when facing North one is approaching from the South – that is, South is behind. In American Indian cosmology, South is associated with Trust and Innocence, symbolized by a child. In other words, an approach from the South implies an attitude of child-like innocence and receptiveness – open-minded exploration untainted by the cynicism of disillusionment. To see the world as a child is to love life for the moment, and not as it might exist at some future time.

Directional orientations on the Medicine Wheel can have a bearing in assessing the meaning of the imagery you (or another person) encounters in shamanic journeying because the Medicine Wheel is of Cosmic origin and thus has relevance on all levels of existence. As a shamanic map it can serve to locate energies and corresponding influences in relation to yourself. Medicine Wheel orientations differ from those of some other systems. Modern-day astrologers, for instance, use a sky-oriented map. Their natal charts are constructed in accordance with a perception point on the ground, looking skywards! It is as if the observer is lying on the ground with his head towards the North and his feet facing South, in which case East is to the left and West is to the right. This is charted with South at the top, North at the bottom, East on the left and West on the right.

In both systems, the observer is at the centre of his own circle of awareness, but with the Medicine Wheel the perception point is at the centre, facing North, with the South behind, West to the left and East to the right. Charted, this puts North at the top, South at the bottom, East to the right and West to the left.

Another map is the Circle of Power of what is sometimes referred to as the Western Tradition (as contrasted with the Eastern Tradition of India, Tibet, China, and Japan). This has not risen out of the tribal shamanism of the indigenous peoples of a large area of the northern hemisphere, which was nature-based and holistic, but from the influences of Middle Eastern beliefs and mythology which are supernatural and separatist. The Western Tradition did, however, absorb some shamanic principles, as did Christianity. This is not intended as a criticism. Any system, whether essentially

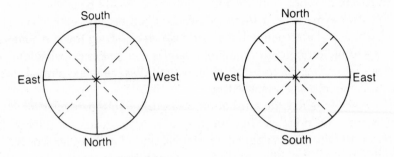

Fig 16. Directions on an astrologer's chart (left) compared with those on the Medicine Wheel

spiritual, philosophical or metaphysical, that 'works' for the individual who applies it, is valid and deserving of respect. I am merely drawing attention to a difference in their roots – one is shamanic, the other is essentially 'magickal'.

Let us consider the four cardinal directions in relation to the four Elements and their correspondences. Although Air is everywhere and can come from any direction, many tribes in the northern hemisphere, and not just some Amerindians, associated it primarily with the North as it seemed to blow most strongly from that direction. They likened it to the mind, which is similarly elusive and intangible, and in a state of constant motion. Air can also be likened to the consciousness of the egotistical Human Self.

Fire, whose radiance is like the Sun's, could be associated with the East because that is where the Sun first appears each day. Fire also has a transforming nature, like Spirit, and reaches upwards like spiritual princi-ples and ideals. It could be likened to the spiritually-oriented consciousness of the High Self.

Water refreshes and renews and is associated with nurturing and with the disbursement of nourishment, so it could be assigned to the South which is associated with rapid growth and the flow of feelings and emotions. Water also has qualities that may be likened to the consciousness of the Hidden Self which can be described as clinging.

The Element of Earth could be assigned to the West where the Sun sinks at dusk when the fruits of the day's endeavours are gathered in. So Earth can be associated with the physical body and with material things. It can also be likened to the consciousness of the Body Self which is constrained and limited.

Of course, it is possible to assign the Elements of Air, Fire, Water and Earth to any direction you like and valid reasons might be advanced for so doing. And every one of them would be 'right' because each Element is everywhere and not confined to a particular area. Putting them in compartments and indicating corresponding qualities and modes of behaviour is a device that enables us to better comprehend these unseen spiritual forces and to come into alignment with them.

However, it is not the attribution of a quality to a particular direction that is the vital principle, but the way it is to be made use of and the direction to which it is assigned affects that intention. In other words, it is the direction of the intentions and the route these spiritual powers are taken that is relevant and not the geographical areas to which they are assigned. The direction we apply those spiritual powers, attributes, and 'correspondences' determines the way we become, for what happens on the inner planes ultimately finds expression in outer physical reality.

Our Earth life is a period of training in which we are each, knowingly or unknowingly, learning to practise the control of energy, in most cases without the consequences of our actions being experienced immediately. In the 'higher' realms, energy-patterns manifest more quickly and are therefore more difficult to handle.

Because energy moves more slowly on the Earth plane, there is a time lapse between the creation of a thought form and its manifestation in physical reality, so it appears that events are controlled by forces outside of us. In simplistic religious perception, events that are beneficial are regarded as coming from 'God' while adverse influences are blamed upon an anti-God – 'Satan'. A more philosophical outlook might regard such outside forces as 'Fate' or mere random circumstance.

On the inner planes, a thought is expressed as energy. That energy creates the events and circumstances manifested in the physical world, whether it is our own personal 'world', or the world in general. Because the consequences of those thought forms generally come into being more slowly on the Earth plane, there is time to make adjustments before they are experienced as physical realities. So our individual and collective worlds are mirror images of 'inner' environments.

We are responsible for the current state of the world, for its development. Violence in the outside world is a reflection of the violence we have inflicted on ourselves within. Envy and greed are inner realities before they find expression outwardly. If the Earth lies savaged and languishing in sickness, it is because our inner spiritual realities have been polluted and exploited by the pressure to obtain self-satisfaction and indulgence. If the planet is to recover, and balance to the environment be restored, there must be a dramatic change in our own attitudes and a new realization of the true purpose of our lives. Western civilization, in particular, has wilfully exploited energy for the purpose of physical gratification.

Although the encircled cross of western mystical traditions and the Medicine Wheel of American Indians are also identical symbols, they are differently aligned. For instance, western traditions put elemental Air and its associations to the East, Fire to the South, Water to the West and Earth to the North. The Medicine Wheel, on the other hand, has Air in the North, Fire in the East, Water in the South and Earth in the West – a 90° discrepancy. It is as if the circle has been back a full directional 'notch' – which, indeed, it has!

It is not a question of one being right and the other wrong; they are different orientations, and they engender different responses and associations. Of course the forces involved are not in reality partitioned within strictly defined directional borders, as the chart might make it appear, and the Cosmos – whether the macrocosm or microcosm – is not really compartmentalized either. The Elements are not separated and isolated to be encountered only in a distinct direction. Each is everywhere; in manifestation and out of manifestation; within and without; here and there. The direction to which an Element or quality is assigned is a means of coming into alignment with it and relating to it. The western encircled cross and the Medicine Wheel are identical symbols, but reveal different ways of experiencing those forces and, as a consequence, different ways of expressing them in life.

We have unconsciously been employing directional orientations to gain control over Nature in order to influence events for our own gain. As a result Nature is now out of balance, and disharmony is evident on a massive scale. We desperately need to switch the emphasis from the mind to the spirit, seeking harmony and balance with all things. The Taoist sages recognized the importance of this when they advised the disciple: 'Do not listen to the mind, but to the spirit.'

The teachings given in these pages are derived from Medicine Wheel orientations which harmonize on all levels, so those same orientations can be used to find your 'bearings' on shamanic journeys, and to gain insight into the relevance of Other-world experiences.

So how do you sort out directions in an altered state of awareness? And even if you can locate directions, how relevant are they to what is happening?

It should be borne in mind that on a shamanic journey the directions are not geographical but *mystical* – that is, they are symbolic, not actual, and spiritually rather than materially significant. On many journeys you may

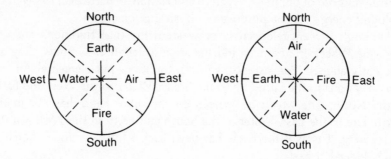

Fig 17. The 'Wheel' of Western traditions (left) and the Medicine Wheel (right)

have no sense of direction, other than what lies ahead of you and what is on either side. Unless there are clear signs to indicate otherwise – such as a sun rising in front of you to show East, or setting on the horizon ahead of you to reveal West – assume that the direction immediately ahead is North, since you entered this Other-world from mystical South on the Path of Trust and Humility. So if you turn to the right you would be facing East, and if you turn to the left you will be heading West. Try to maintain your directional orientation accordingly. If at any time there is doubt just ask yourself: 'Which direction am I facing?' and an indication of some kind will come to you.

Another simple guide to understanding the relevance of a shamanic experience is to bear in mind that the left is the passive and receptive side of your nature, and is also related to the past. Anything that happens on your left on a shamanic journey can therefore be considered to be what is relevant from the past. The right is the active and outgoing side of your nature and may indicate what is relevant to the future, so what happens on the right may reveal what is coming into your immediate future. Ahead of you is what is currently relevant.

Considered from a Medicine Wheel orientation, what approaches from the direction of the sunrise in the East may indicate a new beginning, or triumph over an adversity, whereas what happens in the West or in a setting sun may suggest the end of something or a major change of circumstances. An approach from the South with a sun at its height indicates strengthening, enjoyment and well-being. What approaches from the North may imply testing and endurance through experience, or the receiving of new knowledge.

These basic principles are quite sufficient as guidelines until you have become fairly experienced at shamanic journeying. Then additional factors can be taken into consideration to provide deeper insight and understanding.

On the Medicine Wheel there are four cardinal directions and four intermediate points – North-east, South-east, South-west and North-west – as well as Above, Below and Centre.

THE EAST

Since the sun rises in the East to herald the start of a new day, this direction is associated with new beginnings. It is also related to the Spring, to new growth and blue skies, and to fortunate and pleasant happenings.

The sun also dictates the colour associated with the East – (Yellow) and the element (Fire). The sun is the centre and nucleus of the universe; it is our light-giver and our life-giver. The East is associated with the spiritual Sun – the Spirit at the source of all that is – and with the Spirit Self that is at the source of our individual being. So the East is concerned with the spirit, and with spiritual principles and considerations. It is also involved with enlightenment and illumination – of being able to comprehend what once was hidden in 'darkness' or ignorance.

THE SOUTH

Because the sun is predominantly in the South, this direction is associated with daytime and the period of greatest activity and development. It is the direction of summer on the yearly cycle and thus the season of rapid growth and of blossoming. So happenings in the South on a shamanic journey indicate the growth and development of whatever ideas are being presented to you.

The colour associated with the South is Red – the colour of life blood, and of vitality and courage. The element is Water, which also indicates life, because without water life would quickly perish. Water is symbolic of the emotions and feelings, so happenings in the South on a shamanic journey are likely to be connected in some way with your emotional life.

THE WEST

The West is where the sun sets at the end of the day, and on the yearly cycle is related to Autumn. So the West is the direction of maturity, of harvesting what has been sown and cultivated, and of rewards for past efforts.

The colour of the West is Black, which absorbs and 'hides' all colours within itself, stressing the power that lies inside. So it is associated with mystery, with secret, 'hidden' things, and with death and transition. Thus the West indicates the ending of that which has served its purpose, and the absorption of what has been gained. It urges a willingness to accept change as a part of life, and so prepares for new beginnings. The element of the West is Earth which emphasizes material considerations.

THE NORTH

Shamanically, North is considered to be the direction of refreshment and renewal, and the reception of knowledge and wisdom. It is not thought to have the malign influence attributed to it by some philosophical systems. In the seasonal cycle North is the direction of Winter when life appears to have withdrawn, but when there is activity in the seed beneath surface.

The colour of the North is White, which, like snow, represents purity and cleansing. This is not implied in a moralistic sense, but as purity of intent.

The element of the North is Air, which may be likened to the mind. So the North is considered to be the direction of mental activity and of thoughts, ideas and creativity. It is where to obtain clarity of mind and become spiritually awake.

THE CENTRE

The centre is stationary and is where you are standing in the middle of your own circle of awareness: the awareness of your conscious, Human Self, and of your Middle World reality.

THE SOUTH-EAST

The South-East is the direction of your spiritual heritage: the totality of experience of your past lives which has brought you to where you are now, in this place and at this time. This direction reveals your links with the past and their relevance to the present.

THE SOUTH-WEST

This is the direction to make alignment with your dreams and desires and with the visions of what you would like to be. It is the direction for 'grounding' dreams.

THE NORTH-WEST

The North-west is where to identify the lessons that can be learned from repeated traumas and sufferings. It is the direction of transforming power, where your weaknesses and imperfections can be recognized and turned into strengths. It is where you 'write' your Book of Life through your experiences.

THE NORTH-EAST

The North-east is the direction for the design of energy. It is here that you can determine how to express your life and relate to others.

ABOVE

Above is the direction of the High Self, your higher consciousness, and one of your spiritual being which is connected to the spiritual realm. It is the highest aspect of your being in native American cosmology. Above is the realm of the Sky Father.

BELOW

Below is the direction of the Hidden Self whose function is to enable you to learn from all the positive and negative experiences and thus grow, develop and mature spiritually. The Hidden Self is, paradoxically, your link with the High Self. Below is also the direction of your Body Self who keeps you in physical existence on the Earth plane. Here also lies the realm of the Earth Mother.

My books *The Medicine Way* and *Earth Medicine* give detailed analyses of various 'components' of the directions, and can further your understanding of directional imagery and the relevance of your Other-world experiences. These books, along with this one, help with the 'language' of shamanic experience. Interpretation of the precise meaning and relevance of the 'words' of that language to you, and to the details of your own life, can only come from within yourself. It cannot be explained logically, because such interpretation is not a reasoning process of the intellect; it is a matter of spiritual discernment. My books can help you to build your own vocabulary.

THE TWENTY COUNT

A further aid in directionology is the employment of the Twenty Count, a numerical system used by some American Indian tribes as a means of understanding the subtle energies that are at work.

The Twenty Count is a very ancient system of numerology. Some researchers attribute it to the Inca civilization of South America, but I am told that it is much older than that. The Twenty Count considered the numbers 1–20 in a qualitative rather than a quantitative sense, and though it had many applications it was a means of describing the primary powers affecting the Earth, the relationship of different life forms, and of explaining aspects of the human condition.

The Twenty Count was sometimes called 'the Children's Count' because of its simple way of using two symbols – a dot and a bar – and because it could be demonstrated easily with the fingers and thumb of one hand. A single dot represented 1, two dots 2, three dots 3, four dots 4, and a single horizontal bar 5. A dot and a bar was 6, two dots and a bar 7, and so on. The numbers 1–10 primarily concerned the Tonal reality of mortal and everyday life, whilst the numbers 11–20 were related to the immortal Nagual realities of spiritual life. Apart from a qualitative value, each number had a directional value and a place on the Medicine Wheel, which added further meaning to whatever was associated with it. In Native American cosmology the Medicine Wheel mandala was used as a tool to teach how a multi-dimensional universe worked.

The Twenty Count

0. Zero   The externally existing No-thing that contains the potentiality of everything. The All That Is. The Wholeness of male and female energy. That of which all comes and in which all is contained.

1. .   The power to see. Enlightenment. The power to determine. The power of Fire and of Light. The human kingdom.

2. ..   Bonding power. Transformational energy. The power within. Introspection. The power to hold. The power of Earth. The mineral kingdom.

3. ...   Moulding and shaping power. Emotion. The power of giving. The power of Water. The plant kingdom.

4. ....   Balance, alignment and harmony. Mental power. Knowledge and wisdom. The power of Air. The power of receiving. The animal kingdom.

5. ___   Balanced power. Extended awareness.

6. .___   Personal history and concepts of self. Ancestry and past experiences.

7. ..___   Dreams and desire. Hopes and aspirations. Visions of what we want to be. Striving for perfection.

8. ...___   Rules, laws and karma. How our life is 'conditioned'. Our Book of Life – what we are doing with what we have got and have been given.

9. ....___   The power of determined and purposeful movement. Designed change. Choreography of energy.

10. ☰ A merging zone of the Tonal and the Nagual. Multi-dimensional awareness.

11. ☲ Inspiration and spiritual illumination.

12. ☵ Inter-dimensional organization and stability.

13. ☳ The transmission of energy through the dimensions.

14. ☴ Instinctive knowing.

15. ☰ Holographic awareness.

16. ☱ Access to 'forgotten' knowledge. The collective unconscious.

17. ☲ Power to interpret inner messages.

18. ☳ Cosmic and cyclic laws of cause and effect.

19. ☴ Design of energy unimpeded.

20. ☰ The power of bringing the inside outside.

The above are only brief indications of the 'connections' made through the Twenty Count numbers. It is not possible to provide an interpretive analysis because such insight and knowledge is personal and comes shamanically. The Twenty Count numbers may be compared with the wavelengths of radio stations, enabling you to find a certain frequency and therefore to receive information. For instance, by consulting the Twenty Count Chart we find that 4 in the North is concerned with mental power, with balance and alignment and with knowledge and wisdom, and 14 is a key to instinctive power. So a power animal, teacher or helper emerging from a northern direction is indicative of the ability to have access to mind power that provides knowledge and wisdom in a balanced way. On another level, instinctive awareness may be sharpened so that you can effortlessly reach knowledge that cannot be 'acquired' through study and research.

A South orientation (numbers 3 and 13) implies the strength to put trust in yourself, and to believe that all aspects of your life are working together for your ultimate good.

A West orientation (numbers 2 and 12) indicates practical actions in your life, and courage to make the necessary changes to enhance your well-being through a more organized approach.

East (numbers 1 and 11) suggests an ability to become more detached

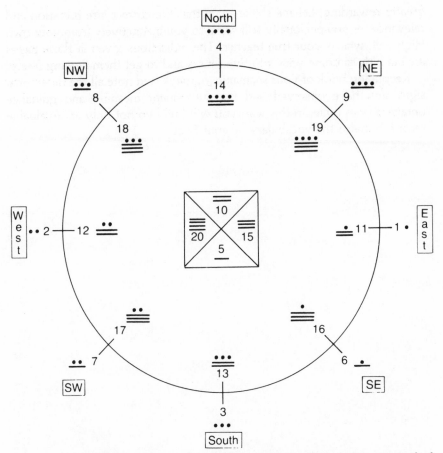

Fig 18. The Twenty Count on the Medicine Wheel. The numbers 1–10 deal with 'Tonal' realities and the numbers 11–20 with 'Nagual' realities

and objective, and to view events from a higher perspective. It also indicates the availability of power to act in accordance with principles, rather than to respond in accordance with what appears to be appropriate.

These, of course, are generalizations of the principles involved, but none the less they can be helpful in arriving at your own personal interpretations of Other-world happenings.

The directions from which power animals, teachers, guides and helpers come and go or are found to 'belong' on a shamanic journey, and thus provide another dimension of meaning to the experience, for they form part of the language of the Soul. As with learning a new language, it takes time to understand and to become proficient, but the effort of learning is greatly rewarding. Let me stress again that the correct interpretation and relevance for you personally will come to you instinctively from your own High Self, who is your true teacher. The indications given in these pages are but aids to prime your intuitive senses and to get them flowing freely.

Keep a log book of your shamanic journeys, and note all the directional signs you have observed and the subsequent meaning and guidance obtained from them. In this way you will build up not only an invaluable record, but also the vocabulary of your Soul.

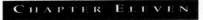

CHAPTER ELEVEN

Communicating with the 'Selves'

YOUR LIFE CAN TAKE ON meaning and purpose. Part of that purpose is a recognition of your four 'selves' and of the levels of consciousness, and bringing them together as a unified Whole. When the four 'selves' are working together as a harmonious 'team', sharing in the same activities and pursuing the same goals, you will find meaning in everything you do. You will be able to clear away physical, emotional, mental and spiritual blocks and impediments, and to transmute recognized weaknesses into strengths, and failures into accomplishments. You will discover your hidden potentials and develop them into practical skills that will enable you to become more productive and fulfilled. Life becomes an exciting and stimulating adventure.

How can you bring about such an integration? How can you consciously communicate with other 'selves'? By getting to know them.

These 'selves' – or what native shamans call 'spirits' – contribute the essence of their being to the total Self and participate as co-workers. They are said to be connected to each other and to the physical body of the human being by an ethereal, fibre-like substance which adheres to whatever it touches and might be likened to the thread of a spider's web.

The conscious *Human Self* – or human spirit – is fashioned by concepts, beliefs, attitudes and expectations absorbed from and imposed by the conditioning of society and by the individual, family, cultural and other influences. It changes its mind frequently as it adjusts to various circumstances and influences, and as it seeks the approval and recognition of others.

The Human Self is here on Earth in order to gain knowledge through the experience of material existence, to eradicate faults and weaknesses within the character, and to develop virtues that will advance the individual towards a perfected state. A lifetime is but a single day in our evolutionary development and the infinity of schooling.

You entered the Earth plane in order to expand what you are spiritually and in order to become an even greater expression of the Life Force – the

'God' Force. Your Spirit chose the body you are in, the place of your birth, and the overall conditions that surrounded you, as a stage in that development. One reason you have been unaware of it is that the human mind, which is part of the Human Self, began recording events and thoughts when you were born. There were no memory 'tapes' of what went on before, that might influence your free will.

In reality, your conscious Human Self is not the physical body, or the emotions, or even the human mind. It is the energy of the High Self experiencing the evolution of the spirit within the human body on the physical plane of the Earth, and for the purpose of even greater expression of the Life Force that is the real you. Your evolutionary progress thus depends on your ability to control the ebb and flow of energy that surrounds you and which affects your life.

The *Hidden Self* looks upon the Human Self as the creator and master architect of the life experience. It carries out whatever it regards as instruction or command, just as an obedient child will carry out the wishes of a loving parent, but only so long as it conforms with the memory pattern of choices, beliefs, attitudes and behaviour responses that have been previously programmed into it by the Human Self. The Human Self and the Hidden Self are frequently in conflict because the attitudes of the Human Self, as it acts upon external double standards, do not tally with those held in the Hidden Self's 'memory bank'. The subconscious might be likened to a chart on which the past is plotted. The waking consciousness is like a torch which lights up only a small section of the chart; the rest is in the darkness of the unconscious.

The Hidden Self thinks literally, not logically and analytically, and it cannot discern between fact and 'fiction'. This needs to be borne in mind when endeavouring to communicate directly with it.

The *Body Self*, or spirit, is in a state of constant awareness. Even if the Human Self is asleep or anaesthetized it will continue to keep the physical body functioning, because it recognizes and accepts its responsibility of being in charge of the physical existence of the human being.

The *High Self* is the most spiritually-evolved aspect of your being – the divinity within, your Inner Light, your god-like Self – the fount of illumination and enlightenment. I stated earlier that the centre of awareness of the High Self is 'above', where it acts as an 'overseer' of the life on Earth. Illumination comes with the realization that the High Self is required to be 'brought down', as it were – to live 'inside' us – to integrate with the Human Self, and become its active and conscious influence through the life experience. Does such a concept negate prayers to God to Jesus, Allah, Buddha, or the gods and goddesses of a religion? Of course not: prayer is an expression of a desire or a request for help to any divine

Source. Any prayer goes through the individual High Self, because the High Self, too, is reaching out to make contact with that which is 'higher' – more spiritually evolved – than itself. Far from undermining contact with divinity, communication with the High Self actually strengthens and develops it and brings practical benefits.

A shamanist acknowledges that space in and around us is not an emptiness but is itself a 'substance' through which movement and change is enabled to take place and communication possible. The language of communication with the Spirit and with the spirit essences of other energy-systems is essentially visual and telepathic. So the 'prayer' of a shaman is not so much words, but a visualization and clarity of intention which is consciously charged with bio-energy through drumming, rattling and the power song or chant. Such contact with the High Self is usually an ecstatic experience which motivates towards positive and helpful endeavours that will be beneficial to others as well as oneself. It extends the ability to perform certain tasks. It increases creativity. It improves the concentration, strengthens the determination, and expands the capacity to love and be loved.

One way of conscious contact with the other 'selves' is through an altered state of consciousness as described in Chapter 7. Shamanic journeying to the Upper World of superconscious reality for instance is a means of contacting the High Self, and a Lower World journey to subconscious reality is a way of encountering the Hidden Self and Body Self.

Another way of making contact with the High Self is through a Vision Quest. This is a pilgrimage to a personal power spot for the purpose of receiving instruction regarding one's intended life path. It is a way of coming into an understanding of a purpose for one's life – the soul's purpose for your being here.

In bygone days, American Indian youths, on reaching puberty, were encouraged to seek such a vision of their future. Before embarking on their Vision Quest they had to fast and to purify themselves. Then, without food or water, they set out to a power spot, which in some cases was located on a high hill or a mountain. On reaching it they would dig a hole and would sit there for four days and nights, unsheltered from the elements, resisting sleep, watching the sun rise each day and set each evening, and waiting to receive a vision of inner enlightenment.

Those of us brought up in a modern society should not embark upon such an arduous task without proper training. Commonsense should tell us that any attempt to literalize such practices of a tough and resilient people of a bygone age would be unwise and possibly dangerous without adequate preparation, training and guidance. It is the principle that is of prime importance, and this can be adopted to suit modern-day conditions. So here are guidelines for experiencing your own Vision Quest in a safe yet fruitful way.

EXERCISE 19:   The vision quest

The first consideration is to determine the actual purpose of the Quest. Why do you want to do it? Is it to seek direction in life? Is it to find the solution to a major problem? Let me stress again that in all shamanic work *intention* is of vital importance, so consider your motive carefully.

Next, decide the location for your Vision Quest. It is perhaps best to choose a place in the countryside which is preferably isolated, or at least where you are unlikely to be disturbed for a few hours. Choose somewhere you already know and are fond of, or go out and look for a suitable place. Wherever it is, it will become very special to you, and you will be able to use it as a power spot on future occasions.

Since your chosen location may be some distance from home, you may need to plan your journey well in advance. Try to arrive at the location during the early part of the morning. If this is your first Vision Quest it is best not plan it to span a night, but if necessary stay near the site overnight so you can arrive there at dawn and spend the best part of the day there. Watching the sunrise in a tranquil place in Nature is a wonderful experience, and it becomes even more magikal when it is the beginning of a Vision Quest. Watching the sunset can also be a wonderful experience, especially at the end of a Vision Quest.

Fasting is a traditional practice. Cut down on your food intake and avoid alcohol for a couple of days before your quest, but don't attempt going without food altogether unless you are already used to fasting. Reducing your intake will demonstrate your determination and strength of purpose. On the day, however, resist any temptation to take a picnic with you. Do without food for the period of the quest, but do take along some fruit juice and water. You can eat afterwards.

You will need your rattle, and a drum if you have one. You should also take a smudge bundle and matches, a blanket to sit on, a notebook and pen, a compass, some tobacco or herbs as a 'give-away', and sunglasses if it's summer-time.

When you get to your chosen site, locate the exact power spot by rattling around the area. Simply move around slowly, rattling as you do so, until you find a spot which the rattle does not seem to want to leave. Then create a circle around that spot using your rattle. Use your compass if necessary to determine the cardinal directions, and mark them on an imagined circle around you using stones or twigs. Then smudge yourself and the circle.

Make yourself comfortable in the centre of the circle, then greet your surroundings as you would a friend. Thank the elements, the rocks and stones, the trees and plants, and the insects and animals, even if you cannot see them. Invite their help on your quest.

Then stay alert and just sit, look, listen and wait. It is important to bear in mind that the spiritual realm uses natural ways and ordinary things to convey non-ordinary messages, so watch out for such signs. A visit by a bird, an animal, or an insect; birds flying in a flock overhead; a discarded feather nearby; sudden changes in the weather pattern; the shape and dramatic movement of clouds. Don't look for meanings or interpretations: if they don't appear instantly, they will become obvious to you later. Remember, you are in shamanic time. Just make a note of whatever seems significant so that you can consider it later.

If you find yourself distracted by the concerns of your everyday life – family worries, work problems, financial difficulties, emotional traumas, health matters – simply acknowledge them and push them gently aside. if after a time you find yourself harbouring doubts about the value of the exercise, accept them as part of the experience and push them away, too. Don't let them occupy your attention. If you encounter boredom, resist the temptation to abandon your quest before the allotted time is up. You may have to learn patience and persistence as part of your growth and development. Don't expect 'instant' results.

You may be fortunate; through the peace and stillness of shamanic time a sudden flash of illumination may come into your mind. You will recognize it when it happens because with it comes the realization of the purpose of your quest. You may be even more fortunate and be granted a visionary experience, which will also be easy to recognize. It is as if the veil of 'appearances' is lifted, and you are permitted to see beyond the physical environment, and shown from this 'other' reality what it is you are intended to understand from this quest. You will treasure such a moment, and its significance to your life will become abundantly clear in the days, weeks and months to come.

At the end of the quest, thank your surroundings for sharing this time with you and helping you. Look around some some small token to take home. A stone, perhaps, a flower, a cone, a feather, a stick … Sprinkle some herbs or cornmeal around as a 'thank you' offering, then make sure you leave the place as you found.

SEEING AHEAD

Shamanists use divination to see into the future. This technique makes contact with the High Self, which has an overview of the life of the person it guards and guides. Divination enables the shaman to receive through the subconscious mind and the Hidden Self telepathic images (from the High Self) of energy-patterns that are in the process of coming into form. The shaman then interprets these shapes as probabilities of future events.

A shaman understands that these energy-patterns are in a state of fluidity and may be modified through intervention by subconscious activity. The 'probable' future can thus be affected, and a deliberate alteration in thought and action can actually change it. Another way of modifying these energy-patterns is through the direct intervention of the High Self as an answer to 'prayer'.

Prayer, as mentioned earlier, is a petition or request to a higher being, and a method of influencing the High Self to intervene in the everyday affairs of the individual. Although the High Self continues to serve as an Over-self or Over-see-er, it does not generally intervene unless called upon to do so.

The words of a prayer are only a way of clarifying the intention, and are really for the benefit of the Human Self, for neither the Hidden Self nor the High Self have physical ears to hear them. This explains why most prayers go unanswered: they don't get through. The message must be visualized or symbolized, and then energized, in order to reach the High Self. In shamanic prayer the conscious mind if focused on a clear mental picture of what is desired. The visualized image is then charged with intention, with a determination to have what is required accomplished because it is being activated by life energy that will bring it into existence. There are no doubts about the eventual outcome. It is not a question of positive thinking but, rather, of shamanic thinking. It involves viewing the world from an entirely different perspective, and being aware of realities that exist behind external appearances. It is knowledge that mana is the vital energy of the creative power that enables things to come into existence.

Mana is energizing power that 'brings to life' a creative thought. It can be likened to breath for it is the 'breath' of life itself. It is needed to 'charge' the mental image being conveyed to the High Self.

The High Self functions at superconscious or Soul level and it is not possible to communicate with it directly through the intellect because it operates in non-ordinary ways. For communication to be established, the aid of the Hidden Self is required. The Hidden Self functions at an intermediate or subconscious level that enables the link to be made and awareness of it experienced consciously. The Hidden Self and the High Self perform in non-ordinary ways to accomplish what is prayed for, though the outcome will appear through ordinary circumstances and in a natural way.

In shamanic prayer, the Human Self (*A-uhane*) calls upon the help of the Hidden Self (*A-unihipili*) to open the way to the High Self (*Aumakua*) in order that the desired result may be achieved. This is why intention is so important, and must be motivated by love.

Raising the vibrational state is another way of experiencing access to the High Self. You can do this by using the power of the imagination to immerse yourself in a flow of light that cascades around you, as described in Exercise 9. Expanding the consciousness by becoming aware that you are one with the environment and with the Great Whole-ness, or bathing in the sound of inspirational music which raises the state of the mind will also have the desired result.

CONTACT WITH THE HIDDEN SELF

The Hidden Self is a separate intelligence within a trinity of consciousness, and by recognizing it as such it is possible to bring these levels of consciousness into alignment and so vastly increase your range of awareness. Contact with the Hidden Self will extend the senses and make you aware of what is hidden to most people. Your perception will be sharpened and you will become more intuitive and 'sensitive' – or what some people call 'psychic'.

One way of contacting the Hidden Self is by undertaking a shamanic journey to the Lower World – to the subconscious realm of activity. The prerequisites are the same as for an Upper World journey – relaxation of the mind and body, a letting go of everyday problems and concerns, and a slowing down of the heartbeat in order to 'switch' the brain circuits and attain a direct link with the subsconscious.

Since the Hidden Self, by its very nature, is subservient, it seeks identification with authority and what seems to be both powerful and knowledgeable. Its attachment during childhood is usually with parents and teachers. In adolescence it is often with a social figure – a pop idol, or sports personality, for instance – that can be the object of hero worship. In adulthood it is a 'god' that is worshipped as being of supreme importance. Regretfully, that 'god' is money or some transient material possession for many people in today's society.

Whilst the Human Self changes its mind frequently in response to external influences, the Hidden Self acts on what has been programmed into it. It acts on what is 'believed' by the Human Self, provided that belief is in accordance with an accepted memory-pattern, for the Hidden Self cannot distinguish between fact and fiction. Fact is an energy-pattern filed within its memory-bank, and it is there in the best interests of the one it serves – the Human Self. So in order to make real changes in your life it is necessary to erase old energy-patterns on which the Hidden Self bases its actions, and to replace them with new ones.

Some American Indian shamans call this technique 'erasing personal history'; that is, getting rid of past hang-ups, inhibitions, complexes and encumbrances that keep dragging you into a repetitive cycle of recurring problems, and feeding in fresh memory-patterns that will have positive and beneficial results. Erasing personal history is fully explained in my book *The Medicine Way* together with a safe and proven technique for attaining it.

The Hidden Self is sometimes referred to as 'the Child Within' because it has certain child-like qualities and needs to be shown what to do. Like a child it requires nurturing and patient encouragement, and it thrives on appreciation. It is also regarded as the 'shy' self because it seems reluctant to let itself be known, and it requires understanding, acceptance and, above all, love. Regretfully, through ignorance, through dogmatism, through a sense of guilt or inadequacy, and through social, cultural and racial conditioning, it is starved of love. Guilt complexes, inhibitions, and other disorders resulting from abuse of the Hidden Self undermine relationships with others.

It is important to recognize that the Hidden Self can radiate only what it receives from the Human Self. That is why some people feel incapable of loving someone totally; they have an unloved Hidden Self. Once you show love towards your Hidden Self your consciousness will begin to expand and the world will seem a better place, because your personal universe has become a better place. 'Falling in love' is an example. When this happens to someone, everything around him or her takes on a more positive look. Days are brighter, work is easier, people seem nicer. The world has not changed, but the perception of it has.

To your Hidden Self, the conscious 'you' — the Human Self — is its authority, its purpose for being, its 'god', just as the High Self appears to be 'God' to the Human Self. Feed the subconscious Hidden Self with love and your High Self will respond to your Human Self accordingly. In other words, as you 'do' to your Hidden Self so are you 'done by' by your High Self, for the subconscious mind and the realm of the Hidden Self, is the 'bridge' that serves as a link between the higher and lower levels of your being.

An effective way of getting to know your Hidden Self is to give it an identity. Western 'Mystery' Schools recognized the value of this principle by requiring adherents to assume a 'magical' name when engaged in ceremonial work. It is their way of acknowledging the Hidden Self and thereby accessing more readily into the subconscious. Give your Hidden Self a name that fits your present idea of its temperament and nature. Not a silly or irrelevant name, but one that will encourage respect and esteem. Sex is irrelevant. If choosing a name seems difficult, you can make a shamanic journey with the intention of a name being revealed to you.

Once you have chosen a personal name, make use of it. Talk to your Hidden Self; you don't have to speak out loud. Talk to it mentally, and take it into your confidence. Tell it what you want to accomplish. Treat it as a friend and companion, for that is what it is. But don't try to force your will upon it. Treat it with respect, and be patient and considerate.

Another way of communicating with the Hidden Self is through the use of a pendulum. This is a shamanic tool which, in skilled hands, is an astonishingly accurate means of accessing into the subconscious. In the hands of a novice its use should be limited to establishing contact with the Hidden Self for the purpose of self-knowledge and personal guidance. Shamanic work begins by first working on oneself, not on others. You will then get to know something of the nature of your Hidden Self and receive guidance on practical matters — especially on those dependent on timing and on location.

EXERCISE 20: Dialogue with the Hidden Self

You can make a simple pendulum by tying a small key or a ring to the end of a length of strong thread, but it is advisable to obtain something more accurately balanced for further work. New Age suppliers usually stock a range of pendulums, from inexpensive wooden bobs on cotton cords to exquisite crystals on fine silver chains.

Some occultists claim that a pendulum responds to delicate vibrations emanating from a force field, but although one can be used to indicate positive and negative polarities of an electrical field, shamans operate from an entirely different perspective. A shaman uses a pendulum as an instrument to provide the Hidden Self with a means of examining what is drawing its attention — that is, what it is aware of — and to communicate its findings to the Human Self. The pendulum is thus a mechanical means of enabling dialogue to take place — like a telephone.

A code is used to provide answers to objective questions which are put in such a way as to invite simple 'yes', 'no' or 'maybe' responses. Of course, any such code is personal, so you must decide at the outset what code works for you, rather than depend upon one that may be given in a book by someone unfamiliar with shamanic work.

To establish this code, suspend the pendumlum freely between the thumb and forefinger of the right hand, holding the cord 7–8 cm (about three inches) above the weight. Use the left hand if you are left-handed. Don't use a long cord because the response will be slower. The motion of the bob — rotations or oscillations — will provide a positive, negative or neutral response to a specific question.

Make sure you are sitting comfortably with your elbow resting on a flat, solid surface, so that the arm and hand are completely relaxed. No muscular movement or mental control must be exercised to affect the pendulum. When you are physically and mentally relaxed and the pendulum is hanging still, just above the surface, put the question: 'Which is the direction for "yes"?' and wait for a response.

The pendulum will swing either clockwise or anti-clockwise, or will oscillate backwards and forwards or from side to side. If a response does not come right

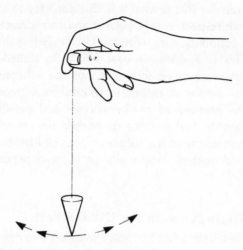

Fig 19. Suspend the pendulum between the thumb and forefinger so the pendulum has free movement

away, be patient. When it does respond, note the direction of the movement, then put the question: 'Which is the direction for "no"? ' Again, remain still and wait for the pendulum to respond. Next, put the question: 'What is the direction for "maybe"?' and after you receive an answer finally ask: 'What is the direction for "don't know"?'

In most cases, the response for 'yes' is a pendulum swing in a vertical direction which might be likened to a nod of the head. For 'no', it is usually a horizontal swing, similar to a shake of the head. In this scenario, rotations are neutral with a clockwise swing meaning 'maybe', and an anti-clockwise swing 'don't know'. However, you are endeavouring to find the correct responses for you, and they may not be the same as for 'most' people!

Next it is essential to confirm the responses you have obtained. For instance, if the signal for 'yes' was a vertical movement backwards and forwards, say 'Swing backwards and forwards if you mean "yes".' Then, 'Swing sideways if you mean "no",' and so on. Should there be a conflict in the responses, start again and continue until they all agree.

Many shamans prefer to use a small, precisely-balanced quartz crystal or amethyst pendulum, suspended on a thread or thick cord, with the point downwards. Before use, the crystal should be cleansed by being soaked in salty water for at least twenty-four hours, then washed in running water, and finally passed through smudge smoke several times. It should then be 'awakened' by exposure to sunlight and moonlight. This can be done by leaving it by a window for a couple of days and nights, preferably around the time of the full moon. Then it should be 'activated' with love, which is the great bonding and harmonizing force. This is quite a simple exercise: holding the crystal point upwards in the left hand, on a level with the heart chakra, think love into it for a few minutes, and charge it with vital force by performing four shamanic breaths to accumulate the power. Blow slowly into it by gently expelling the air from the lungs on the fourth out-breath. The crystal will respond by releasing a flow of electro-magnetic crystalline energy through its tip. This may be discerned by holding it 5–6 cm (about a couple of inches) away from the brow chakra, which is located between (and a little above) the level of the eyebrows. Within a few seconds a gentle tingling sensation may be felt on the surface of the skin of the brow.

Now look intently into the crystal, and ask for its reliable assistance in diagnostic work. Thus cleansed, awakened and activated, the crystal will respond and produce beneficial results because it has been conditioned by love.

Another way of establishing communication with the Hidden Self is to follow your intuition as it becomes increasingly active through your engagement in shamanic interests. For instance, you may feel an inner 'call' to follow a different route on a journey, to take a stroll in an unfamiliar place, or browse round a shop you haven't visited before. Then, as a result – surprise! You come across something or someone who provides you with a clue to information you have been seeking for some time, a book that contains the knowledge you need, or an article that you have wanted but is not readily available. Your Hidden Self is responsible. Act on these 'hunches' and you will soon test their effectiveness. But don't confuse intuitive promptings with the sudden desires of impulse buying, which is entirely different, and which can lead you into financial difficulties. The intuitive promptings of the Hidden Self always have positive and beneficial results, never adverse ones.

CONTACT WITH THE BODY SELF

The Body Self is responsible for the internal 'mechanics' of the physical body: it protects, maintains and sustains it. It controls the breathing, regulates the heartbeat, governs the body temperature, supervizes bodily functions that digest food, store energy, determine the quantities of hormones and chemicals produced, and disperse and eliminate waste products. It operates the body's communication network and self-repair system. It is the Body Self that heals. Medical doctors know they neither have the knowledge nor the power literally to heal the body, only to aid such work. The Body Self is instinctive and guides the elemental forms of life and the invisible forces that construct, maintain and disperse. It is concerned with self-survival because it is mortal.

The polar opposite of the Body Self is the High Self, which is immortal. Whilst the Body Self provides the physical substance through which energy can be exerted, the Hidden Self provides the power – that is, the ability to perform work. The Human Self directs and applies that energy through its thoughts, intentions and actions. The High Self guards and oversees.

Since the Body Self operates at unconscious levels, direct communication is not possible. It can be done only through the Hidden Self. Conscious communication should only be attempted under skilled supervision.

When the four 'selves' are in harmony we feel happy and in good health. When conflict arises and the Human Self, for instance, strays from the path of the High Self, we experience unhappiness and sometimes sickness because the four 'spirit selves' are out of harmony and ill-at-ease.

The Hidden Self is the power within that creates energy for you – that is, it brings into your field of activity the conditions and circumstances you need. If, however, they are not for your real benefit but are impediments, they will not bring you the happiness, satisfaction and fulfillment that was expected. You will suffer the consequences until it becomes apparent that such energy is not in your best interests.

It is all a matter of taking responsibility for your own life, and taking control of it. Not the state or 'society'; not someone else; not even 'God'; but *you*. It is a recognition, too, that where you are now in where you need to be, and that the present circumstances constitute your reality. That reality is an energy-pattern and can be changed by altering the quality of your thoughts and bringing them into line with your highest purpose. It is a recognition that your High Self, as your teacher, will help you to make the best use of what you have, wherever you may be, and a realization that everything around you at any time is there to help you in some way.

It is a recognition, too, that other people are experiencing their own reality, which is not the same as yours. Do not interfere uninvited. You cannot accurately judge another's life for you have not experienced all the circumstances that have affected their inner being. Sadly, the world is full of interfering do-gooders, well-wishers and busy-bodies who are anxious to change it and to rearrange other people's circumstances to match their own, but who cannot recognize the need to change themselves. They have yet to learn that if we really do want to change the world we must be willing first to change ourselves.

Beware of teachers who seek 'followers', and who claim that theirs is the *only* Truth, for it is not possible to reach your Spirit on the energy-pattern created by someone else. It can only be attained through your own experience. Avoid teachers who are anxious to encumber you with their beliefs and divest you of personal power. Purveyors of 'do's and don'ts' and restrictions and limitations who seek to manipulate you have little idea of the miracle of self, or of communication with an infinite source of knowledge, in spite of their wordy prayers.

The situations in which you find yourself have, for the most part, been created by your inner being. Your thoughts and feelings are energy-patterns that draw you to the kind of situations that reflect that inner reality, and the beliefs with which you have been conditioned affect the way you respond to them. If you are not satisfied with your personal world, if you feel deprived and distressed, your inner being is lacking in substance and suffering afflictions. So if want to improve the quality of your life, first you must make changes to your inner life. How? By adopting the natural attitude of a child who is untainted by cynicism and unbounded by the limitations imposed by other people's belief patterns. Understand that you are not separate from, but part of, the divinity some people call 'God' and others know as the Great Spirit — a particle of a divine ray of light emanating from a great spiritual Sun; seemingly separate and indivi-dual, but in reality a part of it.

Recognize that you were given existence out of Love, that you are fashioned from the substance of Love, sustained by the Earth whose face is Love, and held in existence by Love. Then your four 'selves' will come into harmonious relationship and you will find harmony within yourself and with the Universe. Your Earth life is a gift. A gift to you from your High Self and a gift to those whose lives you touch on your Earth 'walk', for the things you do affect not only you but also those others with whom you come into contact. So let your life be a true expression of the beauty that lies within you — of that which seeks to express Itself naturally and spontaneously in Love.

CHAPTER TWELVE

The Shaman and Healing

IN TRIBAL SOCIETIES the shaman functioned as a healer. But healing was considered to be more than just a restoration of physical health: it meant 'making whole'. So a shaman was primarily a person who 'made whole' or 'harmonized'. In ancient cultures sickness was regarded as a indication that something was wrong with the soul, and the physical condition was a symptom of disharmony and evidence of a disconnection between body, mind and spirit. Good health resulted when visible body and invisible soul functioned in harmony with the mind. Shamanic healing, therefore, involves a recognition that the root cause of a problem may be spiritual or mental.

In modern societies shamanists in no way attempt to take the place of qualified doctors. They are catalysts – agents through which required change can take place, and whose approach is a holistic and harmonizing one. Indeed, I have been privileged to meet medically qualified men and women in Europe and Scandinavia whose knowledge of shamanism complements their professional work.

In general terms a shamanist's aim is to help a client discover if ill-health is a result of a certain way of life. An improvement in physical condition often follows a willingness to make changes in an adverse life style. Further, it is recognized that a health problem affects more than just the physical body. The shaman is aware that a human being is composed of several other 'bodies' – vehicles through which the 'selves' operate – each of which affect, or are affected by, the physical body.

The physical body is the province of the Body Self: the intelligence that controls and maintains the body, and functions primarily from a level of unconscious activity. However, the physical body might be regarded as a thought in the mind of the High Self, expressed in material form. This concept of the physical body being a creation of thought is no 'new' idea; it is a very ancient concept, and holds the key to the success of many shamanic techniques. Thoughts are our most personal possession and are often expressions of our true reality.

Thought provides the pattern from which the physical form. The Energy Body which surrounds and interpenetrates the physical body and is part of a human being's auric cocoon, is derived from the initial thought form of the immortal High Self. This is subsequently affected and modified by the thoughts, attitudes and beliefs of the Human Self which are subconsiously projected into it. This Energy Body is primarily the vehicle of the Hidden Self, and is composed of constantly changing tones and hues of sound and colour as it absorbs the thoughts and feelings of the Human Self. The Body Self operates primarily through the physical body; the Hidden Self through the Energy and Emotional Body; the Human Self through the Mental Body; and the High Self through the Soul Body. Where patterns depart from the principal intention of the High Self, or there is conflict between the Hidden Self and the Human Self, imbalance occurs. When such disharmony filters down into the slower vibrations of physical existence, it may manifest as a malfunction of the physical body, or as sickness or disease. The physical body is primarily the province of the Body Self which then responds to the threat against its own continued survival by organizing and directing the appropriate bodily defence mechanisms. I must emphasize that these different 'bodies' overlap and 'join' to one another. There are no distinct borders.

A health problem, though manifesting in the physical body, may have its origins in one of these other 'bodies'. An emotional trauma, for instance, may have triggered an imbalance in the Emotional Body resulting in an asthmatic condition. Stress may have created a psychological condition in the Mental Body which manifests as hypertension. In seeking to restore harmony a shamanic therapist looks to an holistic approach.

It is possible to suffer damage to the Soul Body, and even to lose part of it. In such cases, an advanced shamanic technique called soul retrieval may be used to restore harmony. No one can function properly (and may not be able to cope with the normal demands of everyday life) if they have suffered injury to the soul. Retrieval of a 'missing' portion of the soul is among the greatest skills exercised by modern shamans.

Soul 'loss' usually results from a traumatic situation. Devastating news and deep shock, for instance, may cause the recipient to withdraw from conscious reality for a time; he or she may feel 'dead to the world', or 'beside himself'. An accident may leave a person feeling 'spaced out' for several days, and a bad illness or a surgical operation may sometimes produce a sensation of being 'disassociated' from the physical body – an uncomfortable, woolly feeling. Bereavement, separation or divorce, loss of job, enforced retirement, rape, incest, child abuse – all can cause a feeling of prolonged numbness, a strange sensation that part of oneself is 'missing'. And, indeed, that is exactly what has happened. Only the shaman seems to have retained the ancient knowledge of how to find it, how to return it, and how to restore a sufferer to wholeness.

From the shaman's point of view there are only two prime causes of sickness:

1. Something inside a person that should not be there – misplaced energy which does not belong. This is called an *intrusion* and is removed by a process called *extraction*.

The most common cause of intrusion is through physical vulnerability resulting from fear, anxiety and stress. It is usually due to a life style that weakens the whole energy-system and throws it out of balance.

2. Something inside that should be there but is missing. This is called an *abstraction* and is restored by a process called *retrieval*. An abstraction is the result of a dissipation of energy and a loss of vital power. This must be restored in order for the person to regain equilibrium.

Some shamans, however, believe that a sense of separation, and a feeling of being alone and cut off, will also cause illness. In such cases shamanists endeavour to revive the sense of belonging and of being wanted. In tribal groups, healing in such cases was done by the shaman with the active participation of family and friends, and even the whole community.

A shamanist does not use his own personal power to effect harmonization. Energy from his own energy-system would be speedily depleted, and in certain cases he might fall prey to the very condition he is endeavouring to alleviate. Instead he goes to a source of inexhaustible energy on a spiritual level to provide the necessary power, and is not afraid to touch it and be touched by it.

How does a shamanist determine what kind of therapy to apply? By counselling with the client; by diagnostic work using a rattle or pendulum; by communication with a client's Body Self through a technique of arm pressure; or through consulting his own spirit helpers in non-ordinary reality about the specific problem.

Let us examine these methods:

Counselling: This is not analytical as with traditional counselling. Indeed, the least the shamanist knows about a client before engaging in shamanic work the better for then the client is more likely to obtain what is *needed* rather than what the counsellor may *think* is required. Shamanic counselling is essentially *spiritual* rather than mental and physical work. Analysis is done *after* the shamanic work has been performed.

Experiential counselling may involve the client in exploratory work whilst in an altered state of consciousness under the shamanist's supervision. In this way the client is put into contact with revelatory forces deep within himself or herself, so that both cause and solution may be brought to the surface of the conscious mind.

Shamanic counselling is quite different from western psychotherapeutic methods, for it is based on the principle that the only true counsellors are in non-ordinary reality!

Diagnosis rattling: The client lies on his back whilst the shamanist scans his body with the left hand, palm down, moving slowly from head to foot and back again, rattling just above his own hand as he does so. The shaman listens and feels for changes in the person's energy pattern, using his inner senses as well as his physical senses. When he arrives at an area that sounds or feels different, he endeavours to 'see' with his 'inner' vision what is there.

Diagnosis by pendulum: This is sometimes used as a check of other diagnostic work, for confirming areas of energy blocks, and for determining remedies.

Diagnosis by arm pressure: The client stands with the right arm outstretched horizontally and with the psalm of the hand facing downwards. The shaman, facing the client, puts a question (either mentally or out loud) to the client's own Hidden Self, and then exerts downwards pressure on the extended arm, which the client is asked to resist without straining. The questions are purely diagnostic. Is the problem caused by diet? Is it caused by stress? Is it the result of an unhealthy habit? and so on. If the answer is 'no', the arm will resist the pressure. If the answer is 'yes', the arm will be forced down easily as if weakened. Once a 'yes' answer is obtained, further questioning isolates the specific cause. For instance, questions concerning specific foods might be tried if the problem is one of diet or allergy; naming possible stress-prone situations if the problem is stress-oriented; naming particular habits if the problem is one of life style. Shamans using this method have told me that it is simply the intelligence in control of the body communicating the body's problems and needs to the shaman through the Hidden Self.

An altered state of consciousness: The shaman may enter this to undertake direct healing work, for the purpose of extracting harmful intrusions or to restore power. Either way, the work is performed in non-ordinary reality. Only the effects are experienced by the client in ordinary reality, though the shaman might make use of physical aids to speed the process of harmonization, such as suggesting certain herbal, floral or homoeopathic remedies, or by the application of physical energy in the form of crystalline manipulation or pressure point therapy. Crystalline manipulation involves the use of a crystal wand which is at least 7 or 8 cm long (about three inches) and 2 or 3 cm (about an inch) thick, although most are much longer than this. The wand usually fits comfortably in the hand, with the butt resting in the palm and the tip extending beyond the fingers. It is used primarily to focus and direct energy – much like a laser beam – to energy centres or affected areas. Crystal wands are used primarily on the Energy Body rather than the physical body. They help in purifying the chakras, balancing chakra energies, stimulating the control centres, cleansing the Energy Body of the effect of negative thought patterns, harmonizing the aura, and recharging the entire energy-system.

Indigenous peoples regarded purification as an essential requirement for the maintenance of good health. The principal purification method used by American Indians was the sweat lodge, or sweat house, which provided not only a means of cleansing the physical body, but the mind and spirit as well. Its nearest modern-day equivalent is, perhaps, the Scandinavian sauna or steam bath, though it is a rather poor alternative.

A revival of the sweat lodge ceremony has been taking place in recent years. It is practised from time to time by members of Medicine societies, and participants of residential workshops where a shaman or a shaman's apprentice is present.

A sweat lodge ritual is performed in a specially built beehive-like structure, large enough to accommodate a small group of participants. Its frame is constructed usually from pliable willow branches which are anchored in the ground, bent into a dome shape, and tied together at the top. The frame is then covered with blankets or tarpaulins with a small flap opening, usually on the East side, which is just big enough to allow a person to crawl through. It is normally built by those who are to take part in the 'sweat' and the work – even cutting the branches, and positioning them at the cardinal and non-cardinal points – is conducted with great reverence.

A hole is then dug inside the lodge, in the centre of the floor. This will hold white-hot stones later in the ceremony. A bonfire is built a few paces from the lodge entrance, and this will be used to heat the fist-sized stones which are usually carefully selected from the surrounding area. A narrow mound of earth forms a symbolic pathway between the bonfire and the lodge entrance. The fire itself symbolizes the Sun and the Great Spirit, the white-hot stones the 'seed', the lodge itself the womb of Mother Earth, and the entrance the vagina.

The ground is usually sprinkled with herbs and straw, and the interior cleansed with smudge smoke before the ceremony begins, so that it becomes sacred space.

The participants come into the lodge naked, symbolic of the way each entered life as a child of Father Sun and Mother Earth. At the entrance they are smudged with smoke by the shaman and as they come in they say aloud, 'For all my relatives', meaning that all humans, animals, trees, plants and stones are spiritually related and members of the one great Cosmic family.

In the dark interior the participants sit in a circle around the fire pit, on towels they have brought with them. A helper brings the glowing stones into the lodge on a shovel or with sticks, and places them one by one into the pit. This symbolizes the moment of conception, for the participants perceive the sweat lodge as indicative of their own 'rebirth'.

The shaman pours a jug of water over the hot stones. The explosion of steam seers around the confined space like a miniature tornado, and as more stones are brought in and more water poured on, the atmosphere becomes hotter and more humid and sweat pours off the participants' bodies.

A sweat lodge ceremony is in four stages; the entrance flap is lifted between each stage so that anyone may leave if they so desire. An entire ceremony may take a couple of hours. In the first stage each participant may be invited to express aloud his or her own purpose for undertaking the 'sweat', and what he or she wishes to obtain from it. The second stage is sometimes one of prayer, in which each participant makes a request on behalf of another human being who may be in need of help. The third stage is the 'letting go' stage – the 'Give-away' – and it is during this that transformation takes place. Sometimes more hot stones are brought in for the fourth and final stage, more infusions are made and the atmosphere becomes even hotter. This stage usually takes place in silence.

Healings frequently take place during a sweat lodge, but in any case participants experience a purification and a transformation of their lives and emerge from it with a new sense of direction and purpose.

In tribal societies the sweat lodge was regarded also as a way of getting rid of illness by consciously and deliberately 'giving it away'. Character faults and weaknesses could also be disposed of under the 'Give-away'. It was considered important to banish any problem in such a way that it could not affect or infect others, especially if it was one of intrusion. Since all energy must go 'somewhere' and nothing was 'lost', only transferred or transmuted, even negative energies had to be directed to where they could do no harm. That was part of the shaman's skill.

Highly-skilled shamans – karmic healers – perform a specialized form of shamanic healing. Karma is a hindu Sanskrit word meaning 'the result of cause and effect'. Shamans are aware of a Sacred Law which states that all energy returns eventually to its source, and the human application of that Law is that what is given out ultimately returns. In other words, our actions and attitudes have consequences, though they are not necessarily immediate. In truth we cannot 'get away' with anything. It may take days, weeks, months, years or even lifetimes for that energy to return, but return it will. The shaman understands that some illnesses, malfunctions or handicaps have karmic origins from a previous lifetime, and in such cases modern science is unlikely to effect a cure. Only a karmic healer has the chance of locating the problem, which is rooted in a past life and has evolved with the genes, and finding a cure.

The karmic healer, through his High Self liaising with the High Self of the client, is able to 'read' the record of past lives in the client's Soul. This might be likened to a doctor consulting your childhood medical records. The karmic healer will obtain a clear mental picture of the trauma or experience in which the current problem is rooted.

I have been lucky enough to witness karmic healing. The client was a young woman in her twenties who had been suffering from abdominal pains for several years. She was clearly worried about them although medical examinations, hospital tests, and electronic scans had traced no apparent physical disorder. It was presumed that the pains must be psychosomatic, so she was prescribed tranquillizers. Still the pains persisted.

During healing the client relived a past-life experience which had hitherto been 'unknown' to her. Some weeks later I received a charming letter from the young woman saying that she had suffered no more pain since the healing experience. She said she could never thank me enough for having arranged for her to meet the shaman, although at the time she had approached such a meeting with some cynicism.

The skill required to achieve success in any kind of shamanic healing cannot be learned from books, but only direct from one who is experienced in its use and practice. It is revealed only to those who have demonstrated to the teacher-shamanist the necessary qualities to ensure that the knowledge will be used in an ethical way for the good of the Whole. Four principal qualities are looked for in such an apprentice:

1. A *realization* of the existence of the Spirit and of the sacredness of one's own 'space' and that of others.

2. A *recognition* of the sanctity of life in all its forms and that the only 'sin' is that which hurts another or oneself.

3. A *respect* for the Earth as a Mother who provides the opportunity to incarnate and who nurtures, protects and sustains one in physical existence.

4. A *demonstration* of being true to one's own Inner Light through expression of loving concern in all one's actions.

Love, in a shamanic sense, is a sharing of the experience of life. It encourages what is loved to be joyous, and to thrive and endure and thereby fulfil the purpose of its existence. Love is not possessive, nor does it seek to be possessed. It wishes to be united whilst retaining its own individuality and free will, and respecting the individuality and free will of those that are loved.

The shamanic way is not one of overcoming by force or by suppression, for such actions cause further imbalance resulting in inhibitions, fears and phobias, and sometimes illness. Weaknesses are recognized as opportunities for new strengths, and strengths are acknowledged and modified and used as opportunities to serve and to help others. For the shaman realizes that the way to receive is to give — and he gives primarily of himself — and the way to be loved is to give love.

Illness is not looked upon as an 'enemy' to be conquered and subdued, but as an 'ally' that can further one's spiritual evolution if its message can only be understood and applied. Of course, any idea that an illness can be regarded as an 'ally' to benefit the sufferer is difficult for us in our sophisticated modern culture to understand, let alone accept, for we have been conditioned to believe that illness is a misfortune that overtakes us, and that we bear no individual responsibility for it.

The crux of many problems lies in our current way of life, and physical symptoms are often the warning signs of a loss of equilibrium of the body, soul and spirit structure, which can be restored only when the disharmony factor has been identified and dealt with.

It requires accepting the 'pain' of making changes to the way life is lived. And that requires a much greater skill on the part of the therapist than administering a pill.

CHAPTER THIRTEEN

The Sacred Laws

FAR FROM ACTING on superstition and ignorance as monotheistic 'civilized' man supposed, the shaman operated in accordance with spiritual laws and principles. These laws are of Cosmic origin (for they are universally applicable) and known as Sacred Laws – that is, they are set apart from all other laws and provide guidelines under which everything operates within the limitations of Time and Space. Although these laws never change, they allow all things – tangible and intangible – to develop in harmony in an infinite number of patterns. Contravention of any Sacred Law results in imbalance. Harmony can only be restored when alignment with the orderly guidance is re-established. Knowledge of the Sacred Laws thus helped the shaman to heal, for they are the keys to shamanic harmonization. They were encapsulated in a custom which formed an integral part of native American life, the 'Give-away', an aspect of which I discussed in the previous chapter.

The concept of the 'Give-away' is a practical expression of the Sacred Law of Love which is at the very heart of the Sacred Laws. Throughout the Cosmos there is a striving for union of the Yang and Ying – an urge for the action and passive, the masculine and feminine principles, to unite. It is through this fusion of Yang and Yin that new forms come into existence and growth, development, abundance and replenishment take place. The whole of Creation, in its heights and in its depths, is thus built on the Powers of Love.

Love is both a power – an energy which has ability to perform work – and a 'substance'. A substance is defined in dictionaries as 'a material or essence from which things are made'. So the Cosmos has not only come into being through the Power of Love, it is actually composed of the very essence of Love. That realization constitutes in itself a whole missing dimension in mankind's understanding of both material and spiritual reality.

Love is the power that brought everything that *is* into existence, and it is the very 'substance' from which that which *is* was made. And Love has identity. It has a 'name', though long 'forgotten'. Sacred writings, revered by many, state that 'God is love', but few recognize that Love is what that

'God' *is*. All things were made by That Love and out of That Love, and in That Love we live and move and have our being, as does every other life form which because of it is, therefore, our 'relative'.

Mankind's relationship with the Earth, with other life forms, and with each other, is gravely out of balance through ignorance of that realization. We take without asking, and offer the Earth nothing in return. We deny that the Earth is our Mother, yet our physical bodies are made from her substance and fashioned, nurtured and sustained by her – as are our 'relatives'. We are all in existence because of Love. The shaman knows this, and does not deny it. When we can admit to this understanding and give recognition to the Earth that we, along with other living things, are her children and owe our very existence to her, our thinking and perception changes. So does our attitude to one another. For what we are? We are all made of the same thing – Love. So who do we fight? Who do we cheat? Who do we exploit and steal from? Ourselves!

The shaman observes the operation of the 'Give-away' in Nature. Every lake has its source – an inlet from which it is fed, and an outlet by means of a stream or by evaporation. Trees and plants receive nourishment from the soil and energy from the Sun and give of their fruit in response. The shaman sees how Nature's bounty sustains life and provides protection. Nature's gifts and the benevolence of the spiritual realm of the Nagual are provided freely and without expectation, for they are given in Love. He sees, too, that the spiritual realm does not lose its power through this practice; on the contrary, giving is linked with increase.

The 'Give-away' is not limited to material considerations. For instance, by giving of your time, people have time for you. By giving love, love is returned to you in some way. Thus the 'Give-away' is a principle that affects the quality of life.

The shaman recognizes that the whole of Creation is thus a giving of itself, and a receiving back into itself through what has been freely given. Giving and receiving is cyclic because the Great Spirit is not only the Source of all that is, but the Container of everything that exists. The 'Give-away' is thus an expression of the very heart of the Sacred Laws.

The Great Spirit can be considered as a Great Mind, and all that exists as a thought in that Great Mind. In creating a material universe the Great Spirit put limits on Itself. Those limitions were the very laws of Its own Being, and the laws of mankind's being. These laws put a sacred 'hoop' or 'ring-pass-not' around what has been created and organized into a comprehensive and self-supporting Whole. The laws are what separate Cosmos from Chaos.

My mentors have revealed to me twelve Sacred Laws. I have arranged them numerically, but this does not imply order of importance; each is of equal significance and intimately linked with every other.

Law 1: Everything is an inseparable part of the one Whole.

Law 2: The universe is the sacred expression of the *Will* and *Mind* of the Source and has been created with *Love* and ensouled with *Life*.

Law 3: Everything is characterized energy and is inter-changeable to anything else. So mind/matter/spirit are but different levels of the same energy.

Law 4: All energy in motion follows the Law of Harmonics: it will achieve maximum efficiency with minimum effort, and returns ultimately to its source.

Law 5: All things in the universe have life, but they experience it in different ways. Nothing is truly 'dead' because there is no such thing as no-motion.

Law 6: Everything is made up of the same primary elements and receives the same energies, but individual 'beings' organize themselves differently for they each seek to express an idea in the mind of the Great Spirit in a special way. Everything thus evolves within the law of its own being.

Law 7: Everything evolves by continually seeking harmony and balance with everything else.

Law 8: The only constant in the universe is change.

Law 9 Everything is completely and intimately linked to everything else, and all are subject to the sacred laws.

Law 10: Everything is born of woman. Everything comes into existence through the feminine principle.

Law 11: Nothing must be done to harm the children, for eternal life is through the children.

Law 12: Circular motion is the law of everything. Lineation is an illusion. Absolute beginnings and endings do not exist because there are no true beginnings.

Twelve is the number of organizational stability on a spiritual level, so my understanding is that this is a sufficient number of laws for us to know at this time. These are not dogmas, nor are they being presented in any dogmatic sense. 'Be certain of nothing,' was the admonition I was given along with the Sacred Laws, 'for let it be understood that as soon as you are certain about anything you may be certain you are wrong.' And that, in itself, is perhaps a thirteenth Law, and thirteen is about the shifting of energy from one dimension to another. In other words, when we comprehend that, our whole dimension of existence and life experiences is changed!

All this is a part of the great 'unfolding' of shamanic knowledge which is taking place today. It is happening all over the world, among peoples of different races, tongues and cultures. It is opening out like the petals of a flower after a long, long period of dogmatism, bigotry, prejudice and persecution, during which it has been clasped tight like a bud and protected within the oral traditions of the shamans. The purpose of this unfolding is to bring the knowledge of its understanding within the reach of all whose minds are open enough to receive it. For if the Earth is to be healed of the sickness that mankind's folly has heaped upon her, there has to come about a dramatic change in our perception of life and a realization of its true purpose.

To thrive and endure is the purpose of all life forms. Each is developing through its experience towards that which is greater than it is now. Each is evolving through the pain of change. Each from its mortality is establishing its immortality. That is your purpose, your destiny, your reason for being. Shamanism is thus a personal inner and outer quest that can put you in direct contact with the life forces of the planet and benevolent powers of the Universe to attain knowledge that transcends belief. Shamanism can enable you to recognize other life forms as your 'relatives', so that trees and rocks and even the wind and rain and the very Earth itself communicate with you. For shamanism is an activity of the Spirit reaching out to inter-relate with the spirits of everything else for its benefit and the benefit of all.

Shamanics has no leaders no dogmas, no organization to tell you what to think. And it has no followers, only doers. For with Shamanics you don't have to believe it. Only be willing to try it. To *do* in order to *know*. And then to 'Walk your Talk'.

Glossary

Aether: An invisible cosmic substance from which the physical universe and all that is in it are made. It has a bonding quality that holds within it the pattern of what is to come into existence.

Alpha: A level of brainwave activity when the mind and body are in a relaxed state of awareness.

Ancestors: The Ancestors are our predecessors and our own past lives and are present within us in our genes. Thus the cells of our bodies contain 'echoes' of our personal, family, national, and racial past and have an influence on the way we perceive reality.

Archetype: A universal symbol of an energy-pattern that indicates how certain forces or influences are operating. An archetype is presented usually in human or animal form.

Aura: A cocoon-like fibrous energy-field in which a life form is immersed.

Awareness: Being alert to what goes on outside yourself. Awareness is not consciousness; you are conscious of yourself, but aware of others. Awareness is a function of the spirit and can be active and self-reflective or passive and unimpaired.

Balance: A state of steadiness and equilibrium. An equal and harmonious relationship.

Belief System: A religion or philosophy of not knowing, which rests upon faith in the word or authority of another.

Body Self: The instinctive, impulsive and automative intelligence or 'spirit' that is directly concerned with the functioning of the physical body and whose emphasis is on physical survival. A mortal 'self'.

Buffalo: A natural symbol of the Universe to the North American Indian because the buffalo represented the totality of existence – it was a source of food, material for clothing, shelter, utensils, tools and weapons.

Centred: A state of calm receptivity and equilibrium in which you are no longer trying to meet other people's expectations. A condition of being yourself.

Chakra: A Sanskrit word meaning 'wheel' or 'disc'. A chakra is a wheel-like spiralling power centre located within the human auric cocoon. It acts as a gateway to different levels or planes, and receives, assimilates and distributes subtle energies that are pulled into it.

Chaos: An unorganized state where random laws condition existence. A condition of untransformed power where energy moves freely and without direction.

Clairvoyance: An ability to see energy-fields that are beyond the frequency range of normal vision.

Consecration: An act of setting aside for a particular use. It involves cleansing, purification, dedication and empowerment.

Consciousness: Primarily a function which carries information within a level of existence or from one dimension of being to another.

Cosmology: A system of comprehending the geography of the non-ordinary reality of existence.

Cosmos: The organized intelligence of the Universe and of the whole of Creation, operating in accordance with natural and sacred laws. The Cosmos is thus law-abiding.

Death: A transition from one state of being to another in a continuous cycle of change.

Divination: A technique using a device that enables the diviner to tap into the subconscious and observe energy patterns. In certain cases the diviner is able to obtain mental pictures of energy patterns that are about to appear in physical form. The future thus seen can be altered or modified by a change in the thoughts and actions of the one for whom the divination is performed.

Drumming: A sonic method of changing the frequency on which the brain operates on a conscious level, so that one is aware of non-ordinary spiritual realities rather than ordinary physical appearances.

Earthing: A method of ensuring that after shamanic work or meditative exercise one is fully restored to ordinary reality. Earthing acts as an 'off' switch from non-ordinary reality and ensures that one is fully 'grounded' back into the world of practicalities.

Ego: The part of the human entity that is conscious of being 'I'.

Elements: Components of the manifested Great Spirit that are coming into expression. Each Element has abstract qualities of expression which can best be understood in human terms by relating them to similar characteristics found in tangible earth, fire, water and air.

Earth Medicine: A system of personality profiling, of self-discovery and personal development based upon Medicine Wheel principles and determined by the time of the year of one's birth. It has similarities with astrology but is concerned with Earth forces rather than 'influences' of the stars. Earth Medicine might also be called 'Nature Horoscope'.

Emotion: A flow of energy from subconscious levels stimulated by thought and which can be felt.

Energy: Power to do work projected by a vibratory force.

Enlightenment: Ability to 'see in the dark' — that is, to perceive what is hidden from others.

Evil: Utlilization of misdirected, misplaced or malignant energies contrary to the power of Love and in opposition to evolution.

Feather: The feather is symbolic of the human aura because it gives out impulses of high frequency energy, and its fibres are arranged in a structure similar to the threads of energy that comprise the aura. Shamans use it to align auric fibres and as an auric healing tool. The feather is also symbolic of a message or messenger and may also be used as a badge of office.

Fixation: A fixed belief which the subconscious mind has accepted as a result of past conditioning, and usually accompanied by a feeling of guilt or shame. However much willpower is exerted by the conscious Human Self in the area of the fixation, the subconscious Hidden Self will refuse to obey unless the fixation is removed.

Free Will: Liberty to learn by experience and to decide what to do or not to do.

Frequency: The vibratory rate of an energy field or entity.

Gods/Goddesses: Higher intelligences that operate principally through the mind. They are forces of great power that are personified by humans.

Great Spirit: Native American name for the unmanifest Source from which all that is originates.

Human Self: The conscious intelligence of a human being that commands, determines and makes choices through what information it receives through the five physical senses. It is sometimes referred to as the 'Middle' Self because it operates primarily in the 'Middle World' of physical reality. It is the self or 'spirit' of the individual human personality which has only temporal existence. Kahuna shamans called it the 'A-uhane'.

High Self: The highest aspect of one's being. Some schools of thought describe it as the 'Divine' Self or 'divinity within'.

Hidden Self: The intelligence or 'spirit' within that functions at subconscious levels and whose primary function is to perform and obey. It is sometimes referred to as 'the Child within' because its nature is like that of an obedient child, and as the 'Silent' Self because it communicates not in words but in imagery. Kahuna shamans referred to it as the 'A-unihipili' – the silent, secret self that is hidden.

Imagination: An ability to allow pictures to form in the mind that stimulate the senses.

Inner Light: The divinity within that emanates from the centre of the soul and is an individuation of the Great Spirit.

Inner Space: A dimension of non-physical existence and non-ordinary reality where Time is not constant.

Innocence: Complete impartiality and objectivity. The reverse of opinion and judgement.

Intuition: A sudden knowing that transcends the reasoning mind. Teaching from within.

Kahuna: A Hawaiian word meaning priest, teacher or expert, but when 'decoded' it indicates a highly-skilled shaman who acts as a vessel of vital force which he is able to generate and direct to achieve desired results.

Karma: Life lessons revealed in one's destiny. Karma is a law of action and change in which repetitive conditions and circumstances indicate areas of life that are not working harmoniously, and which need to be adjusted to further the individual's spiritual evolution.

Love: The bonding force which holds together everything in existence. The spiritual essence from which everything in existence is derived. Also, an unconditional sharing of the experience of life with another, which is directed towards the harmonious growth and development of the one loved. Love stimulates feelings of happiness and joy in both the lover and the loved.

Lower World: The non-ordinary reality of subconscious existence. The reality experienced by the subconscious mind and by the Hidden Self at subconscious levels.

Magik: A technique for bringing desired changes into physical manifestation. A process of crafting and shaping one's life. This is not to be confused with the magic of the clever illusionist and of superstition nor with the magick of the ceremonial occultist.

Mana: Vital force that is the pure energy of creation. Mana is necessary for the functioning of the subtle bodies of which the human entity is composed.

Mandala: A universal circular symbol which, as well as being an expression of the wholeness contained within the totality of life, is a symbol of the Self and the Source.

Medicine: The spirit power of a life form. Ability to make a harmonious whole. Inner knowledge. A 'medicine' man or woman is a person empowered with knowledge and healing.

Medicine Wheel: A symbolic device for obtaining knowledge, especially about oneself, and for making connections at different levels of reality.

Path: A route the consciousness can take between different levels of being, or a channel along which information becomes available.

Medicine Way: An adaptation of Medicine Wheel teachings and principles for modern-day living.

Middle-Self: Another name for the Human Self – the conscious intelligence of the directing and reasoning mind which can create new situations and experiences.

Middle World: Ordinary physical reality: the everyday world of our conscious existence. The reality of the conscious mind. The realm of experience of the temporary Human Self.

Nadis: A Hindu Sanskrit word for the vertical, tubular channels located in the human Energy Body along the line of the spinal column and which convey currents of energy to the chakra power centres.

Nagual: The unknown. The 'hidden' and unseen realm of the Spirit. In the Nagual the Spirit experiences eternity, which is a state of timelessness. Nagual problems are spiritual problems.

Nature: The essential character of the Earth or of something on or in the Earth.

Personal History: A strong attachment to a pattern of life which has been impressed upon you by other people and which conditions your thoughts and actions. Personal History makes you feel obliged to explain and justify your actions.

Personality: A combination of character and behaviour traits which distinguish one individual from another.

Pipe: A sacred tool that represents the universe and unites all the human, animal, plant and mineral kingdoms within it. The bowl represents the feminine aspect of divinity and the stem the masculine aspect. The tobacco and herbs are the sacred offering. The inhaled smoke is regarded as the Breath of the Great Spirit. The exhaled smoke represents the intentions and prayers of the one who smokes the pipe and those in whose presence it is smoked.

Power Spots: A place which emits energy that has a beneficial effect on the person or persons there. A personal power spot is an indoor or outdoor place which has a harmonious atmosphere in which personal empowerment can be found.

Relaxation: A letting go of physical tensions and mental and emotional stress and a slowing down of the energy-system so that one comes into attunement with subconscious activity. Relaxation is an essential preliminary to shamanic work and any expansion of the perception.

Religion: An organized belief system in which the adherents are told what to believe either by verbal instruction or by written word. Most religions claim to be 'revelatory' – that is, the tenets to be believed have been revealed by supernatural means. Some religions are also exclusive and dogmatic.

Rune: A symbol representing an aspect of Cosmic power or a primal force in Nature and also a quality of the Soul. Runes constitute the spiritual 'language' of the Cosmos and were neither devised nor invented but discovered shamanically.

Ritual: A method of converting thoughts into symbolic actions in order to powerfully impress the subconscious mind and the Hidden Self to act on the intention and bring it into being.

Sexuality: Expression of polarized life energies inherent in all life forms and especially significant to humans. Sexuality is a process of bonding. It is concerned with continuance – with doing that brings joy.

Shaman: A person who understands that life is in everything, who has direct personal experience of realms of non-ordinary reality, and who is able to function wilfully within them. A shaman is primarily a 'harmonizer', one who 'heals' at all levels – physical, emotional, psychological and spiritual – and in a particular way.

Shamanic Consciousness: A level of awareness which can be entered at will and in which inner, spiritual realities can be perceived and experienced.

Shamanism: The practice of the principles and techniques of shamans, which involves working with the powers of Nature that exist both inside and outside the individual self as both manifest forms and unmanifest potentials. Shamanism is a way of learning by direct personal experience. Its methods transcend the intellect since they form part of the ancient Science of the Spirit. Shamanism is essentially an activity of the Spirit.

Shamanist: A person who applies shamanic principles and techniques in everyday life for the well-being of themselves and others.

Skull: An ancient symbol of the seat of consciousness and of the existence of other realms of conscious awareness that lie behind the material, fleshly world of appearances.

Smudging: The use of smoke to clear away negative vibrations and to attract beneficial energies to oneself and others.

Sorcerer: One who uses certain shamanic knowledge in order to manipulate and exert control, and without loving concern.

Soul: The life expression system which enables the individuated Spirit within the life form to express itself at conscious, subconscious and superconscious levels. It might also be described as a data bank containing the record of life experience. The Soul retains what the individuated Spirit has done with the Life Force. The Soul might also be described as the vehicle of the individuated Spirit.

Spirit: The individuated essence of the Life Force – be it human, animal, plant, mineral or celestial. Spirit may be considered to be the driving force of every entity. Everything has spirit.

Spirituality: Guided power. Being guided in one's actions by the Spirit within. Conditioning by principles rather than by rules or expectations. Spirituality retains the fundamental liberty of free will.

Stalking: The way one pursues and approaches shamanic power once it has been 'located' so that it can be obtained and used for practical endeavours.

Symbols: A means of exchanging energy between different planes of reality. Symbols are links between the objective and the subjective, between one level of consciousness and another.

Telepathy: Transference of thought by mental action.

Theta: A level of brainwave activity that is just above the unconscious.

Timelessness: A state of no movement. Stillness. The eternal Now.

Tonal: The known – the physical realm of mundane, everyday activity. The things you are aware of and which may be causing you difficulties. Tonal problems are problems of physical life. In the Tonal the Spirit experiences mortality and is conditioned by Time.

Totem: A symbolic sensor that serves as a link between different levels of existence and serves as an aid to comprehending non-physical powers and formative forces. Since a totem expresses the qualities of a living entity, it is easier to relate to and is a more effective learning aid than a geometric symbol.

Tracking: Quietly following the signs that lead to where shamanic power may be found.

Tree: A life form which is an expression of a thought in the Mind of the Great Spirit in one place. Trees are in general terms guardians of the environment and of the entrances to other dimensions of existence.

Truth: That which is effective. Truth is what works. What is often dogmatically asserted as Absolute Truth is but information.

Under-world: The non-ordinary reality of unconscious existence. The reality of the unconscious mind. The realm of experience of the Body Self.

Upper World: The non-ordinary reality of superconscious existence. The reality of the superconscious mind. The realm of experience of the High Self.

Wakan-Tanka: The Great Spirit in manifestation that is evolving. The Great Everything. The All That Is.

Yang: The masculine, active, positive, conceptual principle in all that manifests. Represented in some ancient cultures as the God-power behind Nature.

Yggdrasil: The Tree of Yggdrasil of Nordic mythology is the Cosmic Tree of the shaman which links all planes of existence. It is a symbol of the Cosmos and a device to enable the shaman to find his way about the Cosmos.

Yin: The feminine, passive, receptive, nurturing principle in all that manifests. Represented in some cultures as the Goddess-power behind Nature.

Bibliography

Andrews, Lynn. *Flight of the Seventh Moon*, RKP, 1984.
Black Elk, Wallace and Lyon, Wm. S. *Black Elk – the Sacred Ways of a Lakota*, Harper & Row, 1990.
Brown, Vinson. *Voices of Earth and Sky*, Naturegraph, 1974.
Castaneda, Carlos. *Journey to Ixtlan*, Penguin, 1974.
Castaneda, Carlos. *A Separate Reality*, Penguin, 1970.
Castaneda, Carlos. *The Teachings of Don Juan*, Penguin, 1970.
Doore, Gary. *Shaman's Path*, Shambhala Publications, 1988.
Drury, Nevill. *Elements of Shamanism*, Element Books, 1989.
Eaton, Evelyn. *The Shaman and the Medicine Wheel*, Theosophical Publishing House, 1982.
Eliade, Mercia. *Shamanism*, Arcana, 1989.
Galde, Phyllis. *Crystal Healing*, Llewellyn, 1988.
Halifax, Joan. *Shaman – the Wounded Healer*, Thames & Hudson, 1982.
Harford, Milewski. *The Crystal Sourcebook*, Mystic Crystal Publications, 1987.
Harner, Michael. *The Way of the Shaman*, Bantam Books, 1982.
Hoffman, Enid. *Huna – a Beginner's Guide*, Whitford Press, 1976.
King, Serge. *Kahuna Healing*, Theosophical Publishing House, 1983.
King, Serge. *Mastering your Hidden Self*, Theosophical Publishing House, 1985.
Long, Max Freedom. *The Secret Science at Work*, De Vorss & Co, 1953.
Long, Max Freedom. *The Secret Scient Behind Miracles*, De Vorss & Co., 1948.
Mails, Thomas E. *Secret Native American Pathways*, Council Oak Books, 1988.
Mason, Bernard S. *How to Make Drums, Tomtoms & Rattles*, Dover Publications Inc, 1974.
Meadows, Kenneth. *Earth Medicine*, Element Books, 1989.
Meadows, Kenneth. *The Medicine Way*, Element Books, 1990.
Nicholson, Shirley (compiler). *Shamanism*, Theosophical Publishing House, 1987.
Reader's Digest Assn, *A–Z of the Human Body*, 1987.

Rutherford, Ward. *Shamanism — the Foundation of Magic*, Aquarian Press, 1986.

Graham Scott, Gim. *Shamanism for Everyone*, Whitford Press, 1988.

Sibley, Uma. *The Complete Crystal Guidebook*, Bantam Books, 1986.

Steiger, Brad. *American Indian Magic*, Inner Light, 1986.

Steiger, Brad. *Kahuna Magic*, Schiffer Publishing, 1971.

Storm, Hyemeyohsts. *Seven Arrows*, Ballantine Books, 1972.

Storm, Hyemeyohsts. *Song of Heyoehkah*, Ballantine Books, 1984.

Tickhill, Alawn. *Tools for Power, Healing & Transformation*, Galdraheim, 35 Wilson Ave, Deal, Kent, England, 1989.

Ywahoo, Dhyam. *Voices of Our Ancestors*, Shambhala, 1987.

Resources Directory

This Resources Directory is compiled for information only. Any inclusion does not necessarily imply the author's approval or recommendation.

SHAMANIC TOOLS

Britain

John Stevens, 41 Hadley Grange, Church Langley, Essex CM17 9PQ
Coranieid Crafts, The Cottage, Mt Pleasant Lane, Swanage, Dorset
Dusty Miller, 12–14 Weston Road, Stood, Kent ME2 3EZ
John Male, 25 East Hill, Dartford, Kent DA1 1RX
Alawn Tickhill, Galdraheim, 35 Wilson Avenue, Deal, Kent CT14 9NL
Trine Crafts, 27 Filgrave, Newport Pagnell, Bucks M16 9ET
Twinlight Trail, 2 Buckingham Lodge, Muswell Hill, Alexandra Palace, London N10 3TG
Nick Wood, 28 Cowl Street, Evesham, Worcester WR11 4PL

USA

Grey Owl Indian Craft Co Inc, 113–15 Springfield Blvd, Queens Village, NY 11429.
Hawaiian Art Museum, PO Box 665, Kilauea, HI 96754.
Jim Hickey, The Dancing Drum, 619 Western Avenue, 17 Seattle, WA 98104.
Moondance, PO Box 8592, Taos, NM 87571.
Pacific Western Traders, 305 Wool Street, Folsam, CA 95630.
Prairie Edge, PO Box 8303, Rapid City, SD 57709-8303.
Prairie Visions, PO Box 774, Spearfish, SD 57783.
Rodney Scott, Heartbeat Drums, 3555 Singing Pines Road, Darby, MT 59829.
Spirit Song Rattles, PO Box 2063, Taos, NM 87571.
Sweet Medicine, 19732 Potomac Lane, Huntingdon Beach, CA 92646.

Shamanic Medicine Supplies, 9610 Las Tunas Drive, Temple City, CA 91780.
Thunder Studio Drums, PO Box 1552–9, Cedar Ridge, CA 95924.
WaKeDa Trading Post, PO Box 19146, Sacramento, CA 95819.

PUBLICATIONS

Sacred Hoop Magazine, 28 Cowl Street, Evesham, Worcs WR11 4PL, England.
The Indian Trader, PO Box 1421, Gallup, NM 87305, USA.
The Shaman's Drum, PO Box 2636, Berkeley, CA 94702, USA.
Wildfire, PO Box 91677, Spokane, WA 99209, USA.

WORKSHOPS AND TEACHING CENTRES

Britain

Kenneth Meadows, Faculty of Shamanics, PO Box 300, Potters Bar, Herts, EN6 4LE.
Leo Rutherford, Eagle's Wing Centre for Shamanism, 58 Westbere Rd, London NW2 3RU

Canada

Shamanic Foundation, PO Box 2506, Station P, Thunder Bay, Ontario, Canada P7B 5EG.

Europe

European Institute of Transpersonal and Advanced Human Studies, 10 Avenue Berlaaimont, 1060 Brussels, Belgium.
Jonathan Horwitz, Scandinavian Centre for Shamanic Studies, Artillerivej 63/140, DH-2300 Copenhagen S, Denmark.
Pia Skoglund, Alysjohyttan, 5-68096, Lesjofors, Sweden.

What *is* Shamanics?

The word *Shamanics* was coined by Kenneth Meadows to describe a unique process of personal development and life-enhancement based upon a distillation of shamanic wisdom from cultures and traditions world-wide. It is a process that is motivated by the spirit rather than the intellect that extends conscious awareness, and awakens dormant potentials. Its emphasis is on establishing contact with the spirit *within* – one's *own* Spirit – as a source of personal empowerment and creativity rather than dependence on some outside power or authority or external spirits of whatever kind.

Shamanics frees the esoteric knowledge of shamans and 'wise-ones' from racial and cultural limitations and superstitions and from manipulative distortions that have been imposed upon it and presents it in a modern-day context bringing individual men and women into a recognition of the multi-dimensional nature of the Universe and of themselves. Through extending the awareness beyond what is regarded as 'ordinary' reality individuals discover for themselves the meaning and purpose that is inherent in their own lives.

Kenneth Meadows regards *Shamanics* as the most natural and practical way of bringing body, mind, soul and spirit into dynamic unison for the benefit of both the individual and the community.

Shamanics is shamanism – the study and practice of the principles and techniques of shamans – re-newed. It is the 'new' shamanism – a Science of the Spirit for the new millennium.

Kenneth and his wife Beryl, who is also a skilled shamanist, founded the Faculty of Shamanics in the United Kingdom in 1994 as an educational enterprise to further the development of *Shamanics* through research and to provide workshops and courses in *Shamanics*. The word *Faculty* is applied not merely to identify a branch of learning but in its definition also as an ability or aptitude – a potential or capacity to perform a particular skill. In this case it is *life*-skill for *Shamanics* is concerned with the *craft* of Life!

The Faculty arranges workshops which examine and explore the basic principles and techniques of *Shamanics* and a part-time one-year

Foundation Course in *Shamanics* and Shamanic Skills which offers certification. Post Foundation workshops in more advanced studies are available to those who complete a Foundation Course. For information write to:

The Faculty of Shamanics,
PO Box 300,
Potters Bar,
Hertfordshire, EN6 4LE
England.

Or information can be obtained on the World Wide Web:
http://www.shamanics.demon.co.uk

Audio Supplements to this Book

SHAMANIC EXPERIENCE (The Drumming Tape) is a 60-minute audio cassette which gives instruction and guidance on experiencing shamanic consciousness, and provides drumming sequences for shamanic journeys. Its multiple drumming induces a state of awareness in which shamanic work may be experienced.

The tape was devised and produced by Kenneth Meadows at EQ Studios, Watford, England. Kenneth Meadows and Anne Hamilton are the drummers.

Available through leading bookshops or by mail order from the Faculty of Shamanics (price £10 including postage)

POWERS OF LOVE (Shamanic Experience — The Album) is a 50-minute high-quality cassette of a musical shamanic journeys. The composer goes out into Nature to seek healing for a physical condition which is causing her to face her own death. Whilst there, she is taken on a shamanic journey during which she experiences the parallel between her own plight and that of the planet Earth at this time.

This unique musical work consists of the melodies, lyrics, teachings, and inspiration given to Beryl Meadows during her shamanic experiences. It is her understanding that this work has been inspired to touch the hearts and minds of all who hear it so the true meaning of love may be comprehended, for only then can the Earth be healed.

The recording was made at EQ Studies, Watford, England, under the musical direction of John Hamilton.

Available by mail order from:

Peridot Publishing, 27 Old Gloucester Street, London WC1N 3XX, England (price £10 sterling including postage)

Letters to the Author

Kenneth Meadows appreciates receiving letters from readers of his books especially ones relating to personal experiences in applying the principles and techniques he describes. He cannot, of course, guarantee to answer all letters received. Write to:

Kenneth Meadows
BM Box 8602
London WC1N 3XX
England

Or email: **Kenneth @ shamanics.demon.co.uk.**

Index